Royalty Watching

FODOR'S TRAVEL PUBLICATIONS

are compiled, researched, and edited by an international team of travel writers, field correspondents, and editors. The series, which now almost covers the globe, was founded by Eugene Fodor in 1936.

OFFICES
New York & London

Illustrations: Lorraine Calaora
Maps: Swanston Graphics

ROYALTY
WATCHING

by
ANDREW MORTON

FODOR'S TRAVEL PUBLICATIONS, INC.
New York & London

ISBN 0-679-01555-8
ISBN 0-340-41978-4 (Hodder & Stoughton edition)
First Edition

MANUFACTURED IN THE UNITED STATES OF AMERICA
10 9 8 7 6 5 4 3 2 1

CONTENTS

Map of Royal Britain

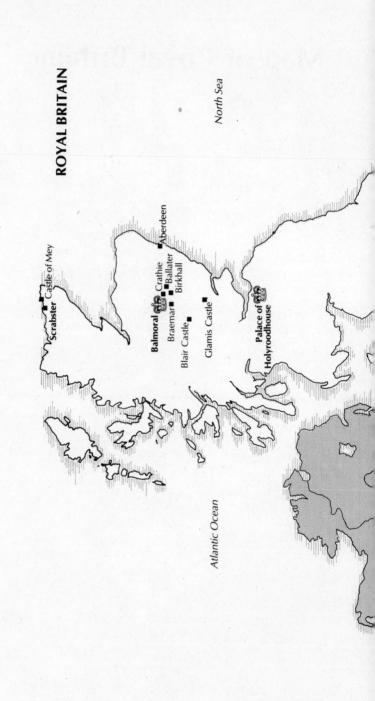

ROYAL BRITAIN

North Sea

Scrabster ■ Castle of Mey

Aberdeen ■

Crathie
Balmoral ■ ■ Ballater
Braemar ■ Birkhall

Blair Castle ■

Glamis Castle ■

Palace of
Holyroodhouse

Atlantic Ocean

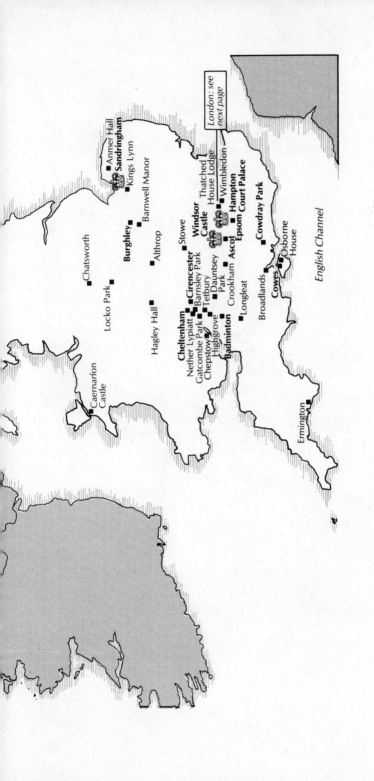

London: see next page

Anmer Hall
Sandringham
Kings Lynn
Barnwell Manor
Burghley
Althrop
Chatsworth
Locko Park
Stowe
**Windsor
Castle**
Thatched House Lodge
Wimbledon
**Hampton
Court Palace**
Epsom
Cowdray Park
Ascot
Osborne House
Hagley Hall
Cirencester
Barnsley Park
Dauntsey
Park
Crookham
Longleat
Cheltenham
Nether Lypiatt
Gatcombe Park
Chepstow
Highgrove
Badminton
Tetbury
Broadlands
Cows
Caernarfon
Castle
Ermington

English Channel

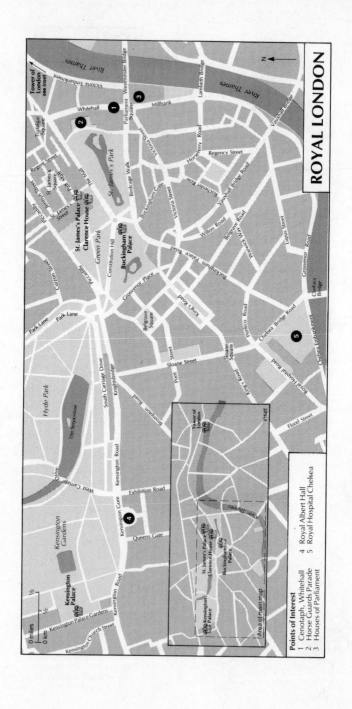

ROYAL LONDON

Points of Interest

1 Cenotaph, Whitehall
2 Horse Guards Parade
3 Houses of Parliament
4 Royal Albert Hall
5 Royal Hospital Chelsea

INTRODUCTION

The two ladies in headscarves were chatting quietly in the corner of a Sandringham teashop. They were interrupted by another customer. "I hope you don't mind my saying," said the interloper, "but you do look awfully like the Queen."

"How very reassuring," smiled the monarch, getting up to leave for the drive back to her country house.

It is this accessibility of Britain's Royal Family—the fact that you can literally bump into them on a beach, race course, polo field, or country lane—that is the theme of this guide.

It is a theme that has had strangely little exposure. The resilience of the Royal Family is one of the country's most enduring and remarkable success stories—in many ways *the* most enduring and remarkable. The family's value to Britain in terms of tourism alone is incalculable. Its importance to the British as a symbol of stability and steadfastness in an uncertain world is immense. Yet vast numbers of people, Britons and visitors alike, persist in thinking of the family as remote and aloof. The prevailing image is of distance and difference. They are seen almost exclusively as inhabitants of that curious, imaginary world that belongs only to the very rich and the very famous. The Queen is a woman on postage stamps, or safe inside a fabulously gilded coach, in ermine and diamond tiara, aloof, remote, and inaccessible.

Yet the plain fact of the matter is that the members of the Royal Family are real people leading real lives. Yes, in some ways of course they are different from all the rest of us, and perhaps that's a good thing, too, if only because the mystique of monarchy demands it. Yes, they do take part in gorgeous state occasions, occasions when the full dazzling pomp and magnificence of the monarchy is unveiled. But behind this glittering facade are real people. Real people leading real lifes.

This is not to say you might bump into Prince Charles on the Tube. You certainly won't find yourself standing behind the Duke of Edinburgh in a supermarket line. The accessibility of the Royal Family has its limits. But it *is* to say that with a little planning and for a modest outlay anyone can attend the multitude of public events—polo matches, horse races, sailing regattas, fairs, and fetes—that the Royal Family attend. And not only will you very often find them there in numbers, you'll frequently find them there quite informally, mingling openly with the crowds.

This then is the theme of our guide, the first comprehensive guide to the public and private lives of Britain's reigning family, the cast of the longest running and most fascinating soap opera in the world.

PERSPECTIVES

The most interesting fact about the Royal Family today is its popularity, a popularity that is so deep-rooted, so complete, and so unquestioned that it's hard to think that it might ever have been otherwise. The family stands at the very heart of the British nation, seemingly unchanging and unchangeable.

Yet why, in our egalitarian age—an age that has seen the downfall of all but a handful of other royal houses, and those surviving as little more than emasculated shadows of their former selves—has Britain's Royal Family alone retained its traditional splendor and fame; indeed, not only retained them, but increased them immeasurably? It was that noted royal playboy King Farouk who shrewdly observed that by the end of the century there would be only five royal families left: clubs, spades, diamonds, hearts, and Windsor. What is it about the Windsors that makes doubts about their future so irrelevant?

The simple answer is that the members of the Royal Family are themselves only too well aware of the potential precariousness of their position. They have long since become skilled in the subtle arts of being loved. The two key words are duty and popularity.

Changing Royalty

The Queen is Britain's Head of State. It's a strange role in many ways, not least because she has no actual power. The nineteenth-century historian Walter Bagehot memorably defined the modern monarch's constitutional role as the right "to be consulted, to encourage and to warn." But that's about as far as it goes. True, the sovereign appoints the Government of the day, but only after it's been voted into office; in other words, he or she does no more than formally confirm the wishes of the people. Similarly, Parliament can be dissolved only by the monarch, but again only at the express wish of the Government or Parliament. Likewise, all laws must be signed by the monarch before they come into force. But it would be unthinkable for the sovereign to refuse to do so. The Queen has no veto. Then again, as Head of State, the Queen has a weekly audience with the Prime Minister and access to all state documents, the "boxes," so called because of the handsome leather cases in which they are delivered. But she can do little more than read them. All she may constitutionally demand is to be kept abreast of Government decisions.

She is, in other words, a figurehead. And who, when all is said and done, really needs just a figurehead, however decorative, as Head of State? Little more than 100 years ago there was a sizable body of opinion in Britain that said, "We don't." The twisting perspectives of history have tended to obscure the fact, but there was a long period in Queen Victoria's reign when her popularity sank perilously low. Her beloved husband Albert dead, Victoria effectively withdrew from public life, overwhelmed with grief and mourning. It became very obvious that visibility was a key factor in the popularity of the monarch. If the monarch were no more than a figurehead, a symbol of Britain, she at least had to be seen. A middle-aged woman locked away in self-imposed isolation made a poor symbol of a nation's pride.

It was the subtle and skillful Prime Minister Disraeli, eager for the reflected glory even a tarnished royal image could bestow, who persuaded the Queen to forsake her lonely role and show herself once more to her people. In 1887, the 50th anniversary of her reign, he suggested she take a new title, Queen Empress, only fitting for the ruler of the empire on which the sun would never set, and ride through the streets of her capital. She did, and her people loved her.

From then on, the pomp and pageantry of royal occasions became an indispensable part of the royal round. It is an astonishing testimony to the success of the royal image-makers that by far the largest part of these ceremonies is either Victorian or Edwardian in origin, though seeming to date from the very mists of ancient time. The Investiture of Prince Charles in 1969 is an excellent illustration. This was a ceremony that had absolutely no historical precedent, but so smoothly did the machinery of royalty run that the Investiture was widely assumed to be venerated by time—an illusion those close to the Royal Family did nothing to dispel. The Silver Jubilee of George V in 1935 was another case in point. Even the family name Windsor, for all its

3

seeming historical splendor, is modern, dreamed up in 1917 by George V's secretary, Lord Stamfordham. Until then, inasmuch as there was a family name at all, it was Guelf-Wittin, a German name, and less than patriotic, many felt, in view of Britain's war with Germany.

The Imperatives of Duty

But visibility and pomp, and the popularity they can create, are only half the story. Relying as they must on the goodwill of their people for their continued existence as royalty, it is crucially important also that the members of the Royal Family are—and are seen to be—beyond reproach. Duty must be their watchword and their creed. The story runs that once, during World War I, sturdy Queen Mary, corsetted upholder supreme of the inevitable duties of royalty, rebuked a princess who had complained after a particularly gruelling series of visits to the wounded, "I'm tired and I hate hospitals." The reply sums up much of the pervading ethos of duty. "You are a member of the British Royal Family. You are *never* tired and we all *love* hospitals." (It was Queen Mary, too, who persuaded George V to give up drinking whisky for the duration of the war as a patriotic gesture, a burden he shouldered manfully but at great cost to his own morale.)

What, then, would have happened if the Royal Family had not been made up of such stalwart characters, always so ready to take on the inherited cares of royalty? In 1936 the country found out. Then, following the death of George V, Edward VIII came to the throne. He was a thoroughly modern monarch, impatient at much royal protocol, bored by his boxes, irritated by court life. Perhaps it was just a reaction to the stifling influence of his parents. Perhaps he just simply wasn't cut out for the job. At all events, it quickly became clear that parties, jazz, and yachting in the Mediterranean with his fast friends were much more to his taste than polite handshaking and exchanging pleasantries with the likes of the Prime Minister or the Archbishop of Canterbury. The monarchy was not in safe hands. Edward might still have soldiered on for all his obvious dislike of so much of the business of royalty (as opposed to its perks, which were—and still are—considerable). He was, after all, immensely popular, and he knew it. But his determination to marry twice-divorced American-born Wallis Simpson went too far. In December that year, after only ten months as king, he abdicat-

The Throne

ed. It was the gravest crisis the Royal Family had faced. Were they teetering on the brink of a new republican age?

The response of the Royal Family was wholly typical. Propped by up the steely resolve of the new Queen, today the Queen Mother, and the ramrod old Queen Mary, the family closed ranks round Edward's younger brother, now George VI, and did its utmost to ensure that the ex-king was kept as far as possible from the royal circle. Edward became, as it were, a non-person, albeit still a royal one. Even his telephone calls went unanswered. The embarrassment and shame he had caused the family were not to be forgotten. The imperatives of duty were restored. The crisis was passed.

This tradition of sturdy royal duty and good works, thrown into such sharp relief by Edward VIII, has been maintained absolutely by the present Queen and Prince Charles. The specter of another abdication crisis and the unthinkable—the fall of the Windsors—has never seemed less likely.

The Human Face

But even this is not quite the whole story. Queen Victoria riding around in a carriage smiling at her subjects or Queen Mary dutifully visiting the wounded from the trenches goes only part of the way towards explaining the ever greater popularity of today's Royal Family. The final part of the answer lies in the Royal Family's immensely shrewd presentation of itself. And what this means above all is its discovery of how to cope with the media. But it is an expertise that was gained not without struggle.

When the Queen was crowned at Westminister Abbey in 1953, she insisted that the ceremony be televised. It was a very clever move. Here, for the first time, one of the great mysteries of the monarchy, its most sacred and moving ceremony, was broadcast to the world. The decision seemed absolutely to herald a new and more open age, the new Elizabethan Age. But it also proved something of an illusion. The Queen knew full well the benefits of making public a magnificient ceremonial occasion, but she drew the line at publicizing anything other than this type of display. The essential reserve, and hence the mystique of the monarchy, had to be maintained. It was a mistake.

It was a mistake because having sparked the public's interest in the Royal Family, the family then refused to satisfy it. Moreover, it also failed to take account of the demands of a new type of journalism, particularly television, one that had a near insatiable appetite for royalty. But the Queen and her family insisted on presenting only their ceremonial face to the world. Never a hint of the human beings behind it was to be allowed to escape. The Queen was seen as a dour, unsmiling woman in a crown. Off duty, she and her family seemed ever more old-fashioned and tweedy, ever more out of touch with the progressive, permissive wave sweeping the country. As the Swinging Sixties oscillated ever more frantically, it became perfectly obvious that though the Royal Family may not actually have been living in the '50s it gave a very good impression of doing so. The problem for the Queen was that she had been so thoroughly immersed in the belief that the monarch should be seen but not, so to speak, heard, that she found it enormously difficult to adjust to a much less formal age and to break the inherited habits of several royal lifetimes and prove to the world that the royals were humans, too.

The breakthrough came in 1969 with the showing of a B.B.C. television film, *The Royal Family*. It was a film many at Buckingham Palace thought, before it was shown, should never have been made. Filmed over the course of a year, it tracked the royals in public and private. It was the private scenes, of course, that made by far the greatest impact. Picnicking at Balmoral, decorating their Christmas tree at Windsor, chatting over breakfast, Prince Charles rowing across a loch, the Queen making salad dressing: the Royal Family consisted of human beings after all, and they were loved all the more for it.

Since then a number of other television programs have followed the pattern established by *The Royal Family*, most notably *In Public, In Private*, two films about the Prince and Princess of Wales. Other memorable television appearances have been the Queen Mother talking about her love for horses, Prince Andrew discussing the royal photograph archives at Windsor, Prince Charles discussing earlier Princes of Wales, the Duke of Edinburgh on a talk show, even Princess Anne on a television sports quiz.

The other major innovation of recent times is the royal walkabout. Prince Charles is credited with the first of these impromptu meet-the-people sessions. Returning to England from his stint at Australia's Timbertop School, he was waiting on the airport tarmac, chatting to the assembled local dignitaries. The crowd grew restless and called for him. "What should I do?"

7

he anxiously asked his equerry. "Go on over," came the reply. The Prince walked over, shook a few hands, asked a few questions of the "How-long-have-you-been-waiting-glad-you-could-come" variety, and has never looked back since. All the royals are now skilled at this harmless and popular pastime, though Prince Charles and Princess Diana are among the few royals who will go on unscheduled walkabouts, much to the horror of local security services.

So it is as a subtle combination of ceremonial and dutiful figureheads—always charming, always correct, always interested—who are both ordinary and very special, that today's Royal Family tries to project itself. It is, by any standard, a winning formula.

THE ROYAL ROUND

The business of royalty involves much, much more than the public ever sees. Both formal and informal public events in fact make up a relatively small proportion of the Royal Family's work load, and of no member of the family is this more true than the Queen.

Her day starts at 7:30 with a gentle tap on her bedroom door. A maid brings in a cup of tea and a plate of cookies on a silver tray. Breakfast at 8:30 is usually a boiled egg and a round of toast. By 9:20 she is at her desk on the second floor of the north wing overlooking Green Park. Before reading through a digest of the day's newspapers, she turns first to the *Sporting Life,* that indispensable record of the turf. She then reads a report of the previous day's Parliamentary business. The Queen has a remarkable memory for detail and has often caught out the Prime Minister when he or she has not prepared for the regular Tuesday evening audience.

After reading these official reports she deals with her own correspondence. Petitions, letters requesting her presence at functions, invitations from overseas governments—the list is endless, though the royal secretaries ease the burden considerably. When Prince Philip read that the captain of the warship in which his family had escaped from Greece in 1921 was still alive at the grand old age of 91 he wrote "Cor!" in the margin of the letter. His secretary interpreted this in the answering letter as, "His Royal Highness was glad to hear that the Admiral was still alive." Friends writing directly to the family put a special code on the bottom left-hand corner of the envelope, indicating that the contents are for royal eyes only. Letters from children asking questions like, "Can I come and sit on the throne?" are all replied to by the Queen's ladies-in-waiting.

As well as the daily mail—Buckingham Palace has its own post office—there is also an endless stream of state papers and documents: the "boxes." The Queen spends several hours every day "doing her boxes," a necessary chore that demands considerable discipline, as Edward VIII found out. Even when the Queen is away on the *Britannia* there is no respite: The boxes are delivered by helicopter. Regular reports on Commonwealth affairs, the Queen's particular interest (she is Head of State of eighteen Commonwealth countries, including such heavyweights as Canada and Australia), are also delivered.

After dealing with her paperwork she will often meet a series of dignitaries before lunch. Lunch itself is normally a modest affair, very often just for her and Prince Philip. But the Queen also hosts regular informal lunch parties for leaders from many fields: business, the arts, sport. They provide a valuable opportunity for her to meet a wide number of people in a relaxed and convivial atmosphere. Lunch over, there is often a public engagement to be fulfilled. The Queen performs over 420 such functions every year, ranging from visiting the local Womens' Institute to greeting a visiting Head of State. Then it's back to Buckingham Palace for another bout of paperwork. She makes a point, however, of finding a gap in the day to take her corgis for a walk in the palace gardens, feeding them tidbits left over from lunch.

In the main, her evenings are her own. Often this means a welcome chance to put her feet up, have a little supper, and watch television. She is reliably reported to be an avid soap opera fan. But every Tuesday evening the Prime Minister comes to call. This is strictly a business meeting, with only the two leaders present. It's a constitutional necessity; the Queen as sovereign must be informed of the doings of her Government. But it's one also that points up the singular advantages of the peculiar British political system. The Queen has been on the throne since 1952, during which time she has seen off no less than eight Prime Ministers and accumulated an immense store of political wisdom. She is not, of course, allowed to express political preferences in public, but with the passage of every year her traditional role as a figure who can, in Bagehot's word, "warn" her Government has invested her with tremendous authority. But these meetings are not all serious discussion. Ex-Labor Prime Minister James Callaghan recalls that one summer evening, "the weather was so nice we left the sitting room and walked around the gardens of Buckingham Palace talking about the flowers and various shrubs and trees."

Like every other member of the Royal Family, the Queen has her schedule plotted minutely at meetings held every six months. Prince Charles and Princess Diana, for example, hold theirs jointly in the dining room of their Kensington Palace apartment. After the breakfast plates have been cleared away the table is covered with a green baize cloth and the couple sit down with assorted officials to dovetail in as many engagements as can be managed, always allowing time off for polo and other royal pleasures. Once a visit has been agreed upon, a party is dispatched from Buckingham Palace to walk over every inch of the proposed royal route, checking timings down to the last minute, media positions, and security. When Princess Diana walks out of a hospital say, or opens a new factory, hours of preparation and years of anticipation will have gone into making the precision of the visit run like clockwork.

Windsor and Co.

The smooth running of the royals' lives—an operation perfected over many years—is entrusted to the Royal Household, an exclusive body of men and women who have been invited to join the monarch's service. They are, if you like, the varying levels of management and workers in what George V liked to call the "Family Firm."

The most senior are the Members. These are the private secretary, the deputy private secretary, and the comptrollers. Below them are the Officials, responsible for the day-to-day running of the various departments. Finally, there is the staff, a veritable army of butlers, valets, footmen, gardeners, chauffeurs, cooks, and housemaids. Their responsibilities include making sure that the family's creature comforts are met, as well as the more obvious domestic tasks. Prince Philip's valet, for example, squeezes the royal toothpaste onto his master's royal toothbrush every night, luxury indeed.

In all, there are around 350 full-time staff employed in the Royal Household. It sounds like a lot—it *is* a lot—but their numbers have nonetheless been greatly reduced during the Queen's reign. There were 458 in 1970 and a staggering 530 in 1952. The pay may not be high but the rewards are great, if intangible: the prestige of working for royalty and the chance to travel the world in style.

Footing the Bills

Finance has always been a slightly sore subject for Britain's kings and queens. Back in the days when they really ruled the country they were forever running into money trouble, much as modern governments do today. Some, of course, were more successful than others, but there were not many periods when the royal purse strings were not being stretched uncomfortably tightly. Yet for all that they were still immensely wealthy. In the mid-fifteenth century, for example, the Crown owned a fifth of all the land in Britain.

But in 1760, when George III came to the throne, the need for reform of the royal finances had become pressing. Parliamentary rule had long since meant that the monarch had been reduced to little more than a figurehead, and it no longer made sense for him to be financed as though he was still the actual ruler. George therefore agreed to surrender all the income generated by his still sizeable lands to Parliament in return for a fixed income—the Civil List. However, he was allowed to retain the Duchies of Lancaster and Cornwall.

This in essence is the system under which the monarchy is still paid for today. Thus, in 1987, for instance, a total of £5,289,500 was alloted to the Civil List, of which £4,326,100 went to the Queen, with the rest of the money divided among the other family members. The Queen Mother, for example, got £375,300, Prince Edward £20,000. Prince Charles, as Prince of Wales, receives nothing from the Civil List. However, as he is also the Duke of Cornwall, he receives all the money generated by the Duchy of Cornwall, something like one million pounds a year, a quarter of which he gives to the Government in lieu of tax. The income from the Duchy of Lancaster goes towards the Queen's private expenses, helping pay for her estates at Sandringham and Balmoral, among other things. But she also donates a proportion of it to members of the family who receive nothing from the Civil List—Prince and Princess Michael of Kent, for example.

Civil List money must be used exclusively for expenses incurred in running the Royal Household. Everything from paper to uniforms must be paid for from it, and the Queen is a stickler for turning off the lights and lowering the thermostat in Buckingham Palace to save cash. "If you are cold put on a cardigan," she is fond of telling her goosepimpled family.

In addition, the Government also pays other specific royal expenses. The largest expense is for the upkeep of the royal yacht *Britannia,* paid for by the Ministry of Defence. This works out at about ten million pounds annually. However, a number of expensive refits have had to be carried out recently, bumping up the cost considerably. Six million pounds were spent in 1986, and a further ten million in 1987. These were one-time payments and should not need to be repeated for many years. The "Queen's Flight," as her two airplanes and two helicopters are quaintly called, are another sizable drain. Their annual cost of five million pounds is also met by the Ministry of Defence. But in 1987 a further forty million pounds was spent by the Ministry, buying two new planes to replace the aging machines the Royal Family had been using since the '50s. Replacement of the Queen's equally ancient train has also been something of a problem. Some seven and a half million pounds is being spent by the Department of Transport between 1987 and 1991 on new rolling stock, all with extra anti-terrorist features. Their running cost, also met by the Department of Transport, is estimated at £650,000 annually. Finally, the Foreign Office also pays out around £350,000 every year to cover the cost of royal visits abroad made at government request.

On the whole, despite the inevitable difficulties caused by having to buy the Queen two new airplanes, complaints about the cost of maintaining the Royal Family are few and far between. Some socialist politicians will raise the same objections every year as the Civil List payments are announced. But the royal year would hardly be complete without them now. For the vast majority of the British there is widespread agreement that the Royal Family represents an amazing bargain for Britain; that, whether banging the drum for British industry overseas or acting as an irresistible lure for visitors, the family repays the government and the country many, many times over.

None of this money, however, includes the Queen's personal fortune. A good part of this, including the fabulous collection of Faberge jewelry and the Leonardo drawings at Windsor, is simply held in trust by the monarch. The Queen could no more sell these than she could Buckingham Palace. That is, she *could* sell them, but the fall of the Royal House of Windsor would not then be long in coming. These royal holdings, in other words, belong

Royal
Car Mascots

13

essentially to the Crown rather than to the Queen herself. The same is emphatically not true, however, of the Queen's own money, thought to be worth somewhere in the region of three billion pounds. This she may dispose of as she chooses. As well as her private estates in Britain, she is believed to own sites in Manhattan and Washington, D.C. But details are nothing if not vague, and the figures remain a closely guarded secret. In many ways, they are truly the last mystery surrounding the Royal Family.

It seems incredible that this same woman, who owns the equivalent of the G.N.P. of many small states, is the same person you might see walking across a Norfolk beach, a black Labrador at her heels. The same woman whose eyes brighten at the sight of her grandchildren or whose face lights up at the chance to show a guest around her stud stables at Sandringham. A woman who will play deck hockey on the *Britannia* with the royal children one minute, yet be engrossed in affairs of state the next.

This, then, is the abiding appeal of the British Royal Family—a family of power, influence, and fame, yet one whose members devote their lives to serve their fellow man; a family you can see wandering through the mud at a country horse trial one day, and presiding over a sober formal function the next.

In this guide you will find the full range of royal events, and discover the private face of the world's most famous family.

WHO'S WHO

The Queen

Queen Elizabeth II is the most traveled monarch in history, and probably the best known. She is the 42nd ruler of England since William the Conqueror in 1066, but can trace her descent back even further, to the Saxon kings of the ninth and tenth centuries. Yet when she was born (by cesarian section) on April 21, 1926, the first child of the Duke and Duchess of York, the probability that she would become Queen of England and one of the world's most famous women was remote.

Why? Because her father, the Duke of York, was only the second son of the then king, George V. Moreover, there was every reason to think that the Yorks would have more children, and that one would likely be a boy. In the unlikely event that the Duke of York did come to the throne, his eldest son— certainly not his eldest daughter—would become heir.

But it was not to be. The Yorks had only one more child, another daughter. More improbably, the Duke *did* become King, following the abdication of his elder brother, Edward VIII, in 1936. The Princess's lessons at Buckingham Palace were prudently extended to include constitutional history and the law.

She was a bright pupil, alert and full of life. Nonetheless, she and her sister Margaret had an upbringing that was sheltered even by the rigid standards of the day. She took her first trip on the London Underground when she was 13, but it wasn't until she was 19 that she first rode on a bus. Neither experience was to be much repeated.

During the war she lived at Windsor Castle with her sister, gradually assuming a more active role in royal life. She made her first broadcast, her sister by her side, to British and Common-wealth children in 1940, her pert voice trilling politely over the airwaves. In early 1945 she was commissioned as a junior officer in the Auxilliary Territorial Service, learning how to become a motor mechanic, much to her enjoyment.

A rare moment of freedom from the confines of royal life was provided by V.E. night—Victory in Europe—in May 1945. Dressed in their uniforms, the two young Princesses slipped away from Buckingham Palace to join the happy throng. It is a moment that even now the Queen recalls with genuine and heartfelt affection.

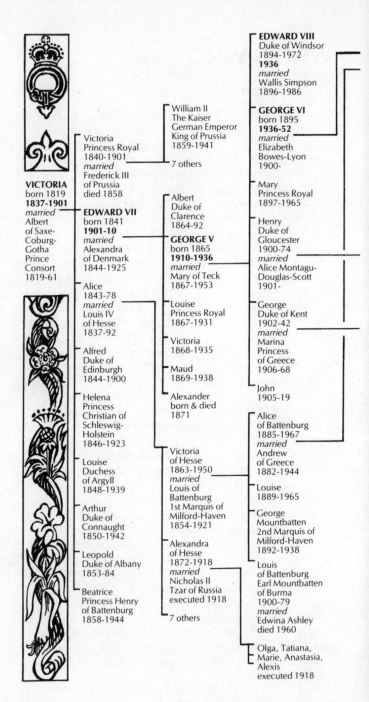

EDWARD VIII
Duke of Windsor
1894-1972
1936
married
Wallis Simpson
1896-1986

GEORGE VI
born 1895
1936-52
married
Elizabeth
Bowes-Lyon
1900-

Victoria
Princess Royal
1840-1901
married
Frederick III
of Prussia
died 1858

William II
The Kaiser
German Emperor
King of Prussia
1859-1941

7 others

VICTORIA
born 1819
1837-1901
married
Albert
of Saxe-
Coburg-
Gotha
Prince
Consort
1819-61

EDWARD VII
born 1841
1901-10
married
Alexandra
of Denmark
1844-1925

Albert
Duke of
Clarence
1864-92

GEORGE V
born 1865
1910-1936
married
Mary of Teck
1867-1953

Mary
Princess Royal
1897-1965

Henry
Duke of
Gloucester
1900-74
married
Alice Montagu-
Douglas-Scott
1901-

Alice
1843-78
married
Louis IV
of Hesse
1837-92

Louise
Princess Royal
1867-1931

Victoria
1868-1935

Maud
1869-1938

Alexander
born & died
1871

George
Duke of Kent
1902-42
married
Marina
Princess
of Greece
1906-68

John
1905-19

Alfred
Duke of
Edinburgh
1844-1900

Helena
Princess
Christian of
Schleswig-
Holstein
1846-1923

Louise
Duchess
of Argyll
1848-1939

Arthur
Duke of
Connaught
1850-1942

Leopold
Duke of Albany
1853-84

Beatrice
Princess Henry
of Battenburg
1858-1944

Victoria
of Hesse
1863-1950
married
Louis of
Battenburg
1st Marquis of
Milford-Haven
1854-1921

Alexandra
of Hesse
1872-1918
married
Nicholas II
Tzar of Russia
executed 1918

7 others

Alice
of Battenburg
1885-1967
married
Andrew
of Greece
1882-1944

Louise
1889-1965

George
Mountbatten
2nd Marquis of
Milford-Haven
1892-1938

Louis
of Battenburg
Earl Mountbatten
of Burma
1900-79
married
Edwina Ashley
died 1960

Olga, Tatiana,
Marie, Anastasia,
Alexis
executed 1918

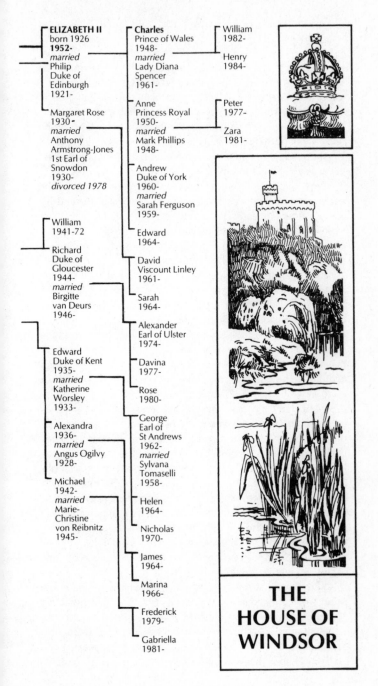

ELIZABETH II
born 1926
1952-
married
Philip
Duke of
Edinburgh
1921-

├ **Charles**
  Prince of Wales
  1948-
  married
  Lady Diana
  Spencer
  1961-
  ├ William
    1982-
  └ Henry
    1984-

├ Anne
  Princess Royal
  1950-
  married
  Mark Phillips
  1948-
  ├ Peter
    1977-
  └ Zara
    1981-

├ Andrew
  Duke of York
  1960-
  married
  Sarah Ferguson
  1959-

└ Edward
  1964-

Margaret Rose
1930-
married
Anthony
Armstrong-Jones
1st Earl of
Snowdon
1930-
divorced 1978

├ David
  Viscount Linley
  1961-

└ Sarah
  1964-

William
1941-72

Richard
Duke of
Gloucester
1944-
married
Birgitte
van Deurs
1946-

├ Alexander
  Earl of Ulster
  1974-

├ Davina
  1977-

└ Rose
  1980-

Edward
Duke of Kent
1935-
married
Katherine
Worsley
1933-

├ George
  Earl of
  St Andrews
  1962-
  married
  Sylvana
  Tomaselli
  1958-

├ Helen
  1964-

└ Nicholas
  1970-

Alexandra
1936-
married
Angus Ogilvy
1928-

├ James
  1964-

└ Marina
  1966-

Michael
1942-
married
Marie-
Christine
von Reibnitz
1945-

├ Frederick
  1979-

└ Gabriella
  1981-

THE
HOUSE OF
WINDSOR

In early 1947, the young Princess was dispatched to South Africa, both to thank the South Africans for their war efforts and to give her a chance to think long and hard about her determination to marry Prince Philip, a determination that dated back, so the story runs, to her very first meeting with the young Prince. Absence evidently did make the heart grow fonder. She and Greek-born Philip were married in November 1947 at Westminster Abbey in a ceremony that brought much-needed glamour to still gloomy postwar Britain.

The young couple enjoyed a relatively carefree life in the early years of their marriage, while Prince Philip pursued his Navy career. In early 1952, however, her father the King, racked with cancer and still exhausted by his wartime exertions, died. Elizabeth, on safari in Kenya, returned home as Queen, still only 25, to take up her awesome responsibility.

Much against the advice of her senior courtiers, the young monarch insisted that her coronation at Westminister Abbey be televised, a decision that did much to underline the popularity of this new postwar Elizabethan Age. But it was a decision, too, that helped set the tone for her reign. While keen to stress the pomp and circumstance of her position, the ceremonial side of the monarchy, the Queen steadfastly refused to allow much light to be shed on her private life, a decision reversed only in quite recent times, and then only partially.

Significantly, the only time in her long reign that she has consented to be interviewed was when she agreed to talk about the Commonwealth, the association of now independent states that once made up the British Empire. It's an institution that has long been close to the Queen's heart, despite the political difficulties that beset it. Indeed, it is in the realm of Commonwealth affairs that she comes closest to exercising actual power. Technically, the Queen's role as Head of the Commonwealth is purely symbolic. But her influence is considerable, as witness, for example, the crucial role she played in winning African support for the British proposals for the independence of Zimbabwe, formerly Rhodesia, in 1980.

Today, in her sixties, her schedule is punishing. She reads dozens of confidential State papers daily. She performs over 400 public engagements every year, everything from opening a cement factory to the ceremonial opening of Parliament. She also undertakes at least one formal overseas tour a year. Thousands of hands have to be shaken—or, more accurately, pressed (it is considered very bad form to shake the Queen's hand; a discreet laying on of the royal palm is the accepted procedure). Dignitaries by the score have to be greeted. Banquets and dinners galore have to be eaten. Presidents and prime ministers must be entertained, first nights attended, garden parties graced, high flyers ennobled, foreign ambassadors received. The full pomp and majesty of the monarchy must be maintained. It is a role the Queen excels at, combining dignity, poise, and absolute professionalism.

Yet at heart she is a countrywoman who loves nothing more than tramping the muddy lanes of Norfolk, with a black Labrador gundog. She is also a renowned bloodstock expert, with a highly successful and profitable horse stud at Sandringham. Indeed, the Queen is a frequent visitor to equestrian events and has made several private visits to the United States to see stallion stations and stud farms in Kentucky and Wyoming.

Her reign has been characterized by a generally cautious and conservative approach. Paradoxically, however, the Royal Family has probably changed more in the years since young Elizabeth ascended the throne in 1952 than in the previous 150 years. But one achievement stands out above all others. Whether by accident or design, Britain's Royal Family has reached a quite astounding peak of popularity under Elizabeth II. It is a peak that shows no sign of declining.

- **Title:** Her Most Excellent Majesty ELIZABETH THE SECOND, by the Grace of God of the United Kingdom of Great Britain and Northern Ireland and of her other Realms and Territories Queen, Head of the Commonwealth, Defender of the Faith.

- **Name:** Elizabeth Alexandra Mary.

- **Form of Address:** Your Majesty.

- **Born:** April 21, 1926, at 17 Bruton Street, London, SW1.

- **Married:** November 20, 1947, at Westminster Abbey.

- **Residences:** *Official.* Buckingham Palace, London; Windsor Castle, Windsor, Berkshire; Palace of Holyroodhouse, Edinburgh, Scotland.
  Private. Sandringham House, Norfolk; Balmoral Castle, Aberdeenshire, Scotland.

- **Children:** HRH THE PRINCE OF WALES (Charles Philip Arthur George), born November 14, 1948.
  HRH THE PRINCESS ROYAL (Anne Elizabeth Alice Louise), born August 15, 1950.

HRH THE DUKE OF YORK (Andrew Albert Christian Edward),
born February 19, 1960.

HRH PRINCE EDWARD (Antony Richard Louis), born March 10,
1964.

● **_Interests:_** Racing, gundog and bloodstock breeding, jigsaw puzzles.

Prince Philip

"I have no axe to grind and nothing to sell. The line I take is my
own," says Prince Philip, the Duke of Edinburgh, the Queen's
consort and professional headline maker.

Tough-minded, irascible, impatient, and eternally restless,
Prince Philip has decisively influenced the way the British monarchy has faced the daunting challenges of the postwar world.
Indeed, the fact that Britain's Royal Family has not only survived
unscathed a period when dozens of other royal families around
the world have fallen but has vastly increased its popularity is
a cogent measure of his success. For while the Queen has spent
much time on affairs of state, the Duke of Edinburgh has con-
centrated his enormous energies on shaping and adapting the
"Family Firm," as George V called the Royal Family.

Thus the Prince has revolutionized business practices on the
royal estates at Sandringham and Balmoral. Likewise, he put in
place much innovative reorganization at Buckingham Palace.
Early in the Queen's reign, he also took an active interest in the
design and construction of the new royal yacht, _Britannia_—an
appropriate activity given his background as a career naval
officer.

At the same time, he and the Queen successfully faced up to
the potentially vexing problems of educating their children,
ensuring that their childhoods were as normal as possible while
yet inculcating in them a strong sense of their historic responsibilities, the necessary duties that attended their privileged
births. Inevitably, there was criticism, with the royal couple
variously accused of being either too liberal or, more convinc-
ingly, too strict with their children.

Yet Prince Philip's world could have been so very different.
He was born Prince Philip of Greece on the Mediterranean
island of Corfu on June 10, 1921, the son of Prince Andrew of
Greece (who despite his title, and indeed the fact that his broth-
er was King Constantine of Greece, was no more Greek than old
Queen Victoria had been, as his family name of Schleswig-
Holstein-Sonderburg-Gluckburg made only too clear) and Prin-

cess Alice, herself a granddaughter of Queen Victoria. Eighteen months later, the Greek royal family, a shaky, indeed largely bogus institution, collapsed, a fall precipitated by a disastrous military campaign against neighboring Turkey led by Prince Andrew.

Haunted by the fall and eventual murder of another set of royal cousins—the Romanovs of Russia—George V persuaded his government to rescue his Greek relations. Thus the infant Prince Philip sailed into exile in an orange box on the deck of a Royal Navy warship, H.M.S. *Calypso*. He was welcomed rather cautiously by the Royal Family—his parents were separated and impoverished—and his early life in Britain was rootless. He found himself transferred from one royal household to another, finally settling under the wing of his ambitious and clever uncle, Lord Mountbatten, affectionately known as Uncle Dickie, himself a professional sailor and later to be the last viceroy of India.

The Prince joined one of the first classes at Gordonstoun, German Kurt Hahn's unorthodox school in the north of Scotland. He was an outstanding all-rounder at the school, shining at sailing, athletics, cricket, and hockey. From Gordonstoun, the Prince joined the Royal Navy, a decision that owed much to his Uncle Dickie's persuasive influence.

It was while at Dartmouth College, the Navy's training school, that he first met the young Princess Elizabeth, his third cousin. Legend has it that the Princess was so smitten by the dashing cadet that she set her heart on marriage there and then although only 13. Legend also has it that Uncle Dickie had shrewdly foreseen the possibility of royal romance blossoming —a romance that would do much to enhance his own prestige at court—and had taken every step to encourage it.

During the war, the Prince saw action at the naval battle off Cape Matapan—ironically in Greek waters—an engagement that led to his being mentioned in dispatches. But his romance with Princess Elizabeth was far from plain sailing. The problem was not that anyone doubted the love the young couple bore one another. Rather, despite his impeccable royal background, the Prince remained technically a Greek citizen, and Greece was currently racked by a vicious civil war. Additionally, though less publicized, there were delicate problems posed by the fact that all Prince Philip's sisters had married Germans, two of whom had lately served with enthusiasm in the Nazi armed

21

forces. It hardly amounted to a suitable background for a potential consort of the heir to the British throne.

Real though these stumbling blocks were, they were nonetheless all neatly sidestepped. First, the Prince changed his nationality, becoming a British citizen and in the process taking his uncle's surname, Mountbatten. Second, the Princess was determined to marry the man of her dreams, and emphatically swept aside objections concerning his antecedents. When the wedding finally took place, his sisters were simply not invited.

Following their marriage, the Prince returned to the Navy, a career that seemed tailor-made for his cheerful, outgoing personality. But his maritime ambitions were dashed on the death of George VI in 1952. It's no secret that he found the task of adjusting from Navy life to full-time court life painful at times, not least because he had no actual role to play beyond acting, in a memorable phrase, "as a handsome clothes-horse for the uniforms he wore so well on ceremonial occasions." But the Prince coped in typically forthright fashion, throwing himself wholeheartedly into causes dear to his heart. A series of trenchant speeches established the typical Prince Philip style: commonsensical and practical, his salty language a bracing blast of fresh air in comparison to the anodyne bromides royals normally utter.

There have been times when the Prince's blunt, no-nonsense approach has strayed perilously close to the downright tactless, a characteristic shared by his daughter Anne. Yet his popularity has never been questioned. His major concerns have been the encouragement of sport among the young, and conservation and the environment. His Duke of Edinburgh Scheme, which gives youngsters the chance to develop a variety of abilities, celebrated its 31st anniversary in 1987. He has been an active president of the World Wildlife Fund, although critics have not been slow to point to the incongruity of his love of shooting and his simultaneous championing of wildlife preservation.

He has also long been an avid polo enthusiast, a sport he gave up only reluctantly following the onset of arthritis. However, he transferred his equine interests successfully to the fast developing sport of carriage driving, achieving considerable success as a competitor and establishing his own carriage-driving school on the Sandringham estate.

Yet of all his many interests and achievements, the Prince will probably be best remembered as the catalyst for both change and, crucially, stability within the Royal Family.

- **Title:** His Royal Highness THE PRINCE PHILIP, Duke of Edinburgh, Earl of Merioneth, and Baron Greenwich.

- **Form of Address:** Your Royal Highness.

- **Born:** June 10, 1921, on the island of Corfu, Greece.

- **Married:** November 20, 1947, at Westminster Abbey.

- **Residences:** *Official.* Buckingham Palace, London; Windsor Castle, Windsor, Berkshire; Palace of Hoyroodhouse, Edinburgh, Scotland.
  Private. Sandringham House, Norfolk; Balmoral Castle, Aberdeenshire, Scotland.

- **Honors:** Knight of the Garter; Knight of the Thistle; Privy Councillor; Order of Merit; Knight Grand Cross of the Order of the British Empire.

- **Principal Patronages:** Chancellor, Universities of Edinburgh, Cambridge, and Salford; Life Governor, King's College, London; Admiral of the Fleet; Field Marshall; Marshall of the Royal Air Force; Admiral, Royal Yacht Squadron; Grand Master, Guild of Air Pilots and Air Navigators; Master of the Corporation of Trinity House; Ranger of Windsor Park; president, World Wildlife Fund International, and International Equestrian Federation.

- **Publications:** *Selected Speeches 1948–55* (1957); *Prince Philip Speaks* (1960); *Birds from Britannia* (1962); *Wildlife Crisis* (with James Fisher, 1970); *The Environmental Revolution* (1978); *A Question of Balance* (1982); *Competition Carriage Driving* (1982); *Men, Machines and Sacred Cows* (1984).

- **Interests:** Equestrianism, sailing, carriage driving, and polo.

- **Sport:** Member, British carriage-driving team since 1975 (International Gold Medal, 1980); winning owner (Camira Flash), 1968 Greyhound Derby; captain, Windsor Park polo team, 1955–71; many wins in Dragon and Flying 15 racing dinghies, 1948–62; frequent competitor in yawl *Bloodhound* (1962–69); captain of cricket at Gordonstoun, 1938; president, Marylebone Cricket Club, 1949–50, 1974–75.

The Prince of Wales

Prince Charles has one of the most difficult positions in the world. He has a role but not a job, influence but no power, and duties but few rights. When he finally becomes King Charles III, he is likely to be in his mid sixties, the bulk of his adult life spent in simply waiting for his destiny to be fulfilled.

It's a problem he has long recognized. It accounts at least in part for his insistence on devoting so much of his time to Prince William, his elder son and second in line to the throne. But in addition to teaching his son the obligations—and the problems —that accompany his position, the Prince has been concerned that both William and his brother, Prince Harry, should not suffer the lonely and isolated childhood he endured.

Charles Philip Arthur George was born at Buckingham Palace on Sunday, November 14, 1948, the first child of Princess Elizabeth and Prince Philip. His upbringing was a combination of the traditional and the innovative. For the first years of his life he was brought up in the Buckingham Palace nursery, under the watchful eye of nurse Helen Lightbody.

The Queen and Prince Philip then took the unprecedented step of sending their son, the future King, to an ordinary school, Hill House, in London's Knightsbridge. From there he was sent to Cheam Preparatory School, following in his father's foot-steps. It was an experiment that very nearly failed. Anxious to shield their son from the press, the Royal Family inadvertently succeeded only in stirring up interest in the young Prince to fever pitch. Numerous journalists and photographers were found lurking on the grounds of the school. Eventually, the Queen found herself obliged to issue a formal warning to the effect that Charles would be removed from the school unless he was allowed to continue his time there in peace.

From Cheam, Prince Charles was sent, again somewhat con-troversially, to Gordonstoun, once more following in his father's footsteps. The tough, spartan conditions at the school may have suited extrovert Prince Philip, but Charles "hated" his time there, though he duly became head boy, and took the leading part in a school production of Macbeth.

Far more enjoyable were two terms he subsequently spent in Australia, at Timbertop School near Melbourne. Thereafter, Charles continued his education at Trinity College, Cambridge, where he studied history and played the cello (passably).

This was perhaps the Prince's most difficult and awkward period. He attended Cambridge at the height of the student upheavals of the late '60s, yet cut less than a dash in his tweed jackets and sensible shoes. There was a sense of his having become curiously detached from his time. He gave the strong impression that he would have been far more at home in the '50s rather than the radical, chic '60s. There was little hint of the quietly confident man of the world the Prince was to become.

Nonetheless, the Prince entered into college life with as much gusto as could reasonably be expected, notably taking part in a number of college satirical revues. His time at Cambridge was interrupted in 1969 by his Investiture as Prince of Wales in an elaborate and nerve-wracking ceremony at Caernarfon Castle, a ceremony that did much to restore the flagging image of the Royal Family and to boost the popularity of the Prince to new heights.

From Cambridge, the Prince followed the well-trodden royal route into the armed forces, joining in turn the R.A.F. and the Royal Navy. He ended his time in the Navy in command of a minesweeper, H.M.S. *Bronington*. It was a period of increasing maturity for the Prince, one he evidently regards with some affection, not least perhaps for having been allowed to escape the otherwise constant attentions of the press. A measure of the affection he in turn inspired in his men is the name they coined for him, Taffy Windsor.

Leaving the Navy, the Prince, by now probably the most popular member of the Royal Family, performed his royal duties valiantly. Yet there remained a sense, at least until his marriage to Lady Diana Spencer in 1981, of a certain dissatisfaction with his lot, of an aimlessness in his life. Perhaps this was no more than the natural reaction of a man of sensitivity and intelligence to the permanent glare of media interest, particularly the obsessive interest in his girlfriends (of which there was no shortage). Being repeatedly labeled the most eligible bachelor in the world is scarcely an enviable state, however assiduously you may have been trained to deal with it. Yet a measure of his sincere desire to help the disadvantaged and unemployed, especially among the young, is provided by the trusts he has established, many of them highly successful.

Since his marriage he has seemed more settled and content, if rather less approachable. The days when he would wear a funny nose for photographers are gone forever. His interests are wide-reaching, embracing everything from inner-city decay, alternative medicine, and "community" architecture to Buddhism and Jungian philosophy. However, like his father, polo takes precedence over philosophy in the summer.

While not overtly political, the Prince has made a number of hard-hitting speeches on the nation's ills. Some powerful consciences have been pricked by his occasionally fierce attacks, and much-needed public debate has been produced. He has also undertaken a number of arduous overseas tours, losing no opportunity to promote British industry in the process, and has shown himself to be an astute ambassador for his country.

In these and many other ways, he is carving for himself a useful role in public life as he waits patiently for his real job to begin. He may well have to wait several decades longer.

- **Title:** His Royal Highness THE PRINCE OF WALES.

- **Name:** Charles Philip Arthur George.

- **Form of Address:** Your Royal Highness.

- **Born:** November 14, 1948, at Buckingham Palace, London.

- **Married:** July 29, 1981, at St. Paul's Cathedral.

- **Residences:** Kensington Palace, London; Highgrove, Tetbury, Gloucestershire; Tamarisk, St. Mary's, Isles of Scilly.

- **Honors:** Heir to the Throne; Prince of Wales; Earl of Chester; Duke of Cornwall; Duke of Rothesay; Earl of Carrick; Baron Renfrew; Lord of the Isles; Great Steward of Scotland; Knight of the Garter; Knight of the Thistle; Knight Grand Cross of the Order of the Bath; Privy Councillor; Personal A.D.C. to the Queen.

- **Principal Patronages:** Chancellor, University of Wales; Colonel-in-Chief, Cheshire Regiment, Gordon Highlanders, and Parachute Regiment; Great Master of the Order of the Bath; Honorary Bencher, Gray's Inn; president, United World Colleges, and the Prince's Trust; chairman, Queen's Silver Jubilee Trust, and Prince of Wales' Committee for Wales; patron, Press Club, Welsh National Opera, Royal School for the Blind, and *Mary Rose* Trust; Commodore, Royal Thames Yacht Club; High Steward, Royal Borough of Windsor and Maidenhead.

- **Publication:** *The Old Man of Lochnagar* (1983).

- **Interests:** Polo, music, gardening, painting, alternative medicine, and collecting antique lavatory seats.

Princess Diana

Princess Diana, the Princess of Wales, has transformed the modern image of the Royal Family in a way that no other single figure or event has come even close to doing. Since her arrival on the royal scene in an explosion of publicity in 1981, interest in the Royal Family, already strong, has become intense and unwavering.

The Princess has brought a charisma and glamour, a freshness and appeal to royal life, enabling the British Royal Family to transcend barriers the world over. It's a fair bet she is now better known than her mother-in-law. The plain fact is that there are millions of people from all corners of the globe who will wait hours to catch no more than just a glimpse of her.

The Princess of Wales, the former Lady Diana Spencer, was born on July 1, 1961, the daughter of the then Lord and Lady Althorp, today Earl Spencer and the Honorable Mrs. Frances Shand-Kydd. Surprisingly, she is the first Englishwoman to marry an heir to the throne for 300 years (Germans and Danes have predominated). Although not of royal blood, her family has been linked to the great houses of England for centuries. She descends no less than five times from the illegitimate children of Charles II, thereby reintroducing Stuart blood to the Royal Family for the first time since the accession of William of Orange in 1689. For what it's worth, genealogists have also managed to trace her family links to George Washington, Humphrey Bogart, and Rudolph Valentino, among others.

She was brought up in her father's house on the Queen's estate at Sandringham, where among her earliest playmates were Prince Andrew and Prince Edward. As a teenager, she joked that one day she would marry Prince Andrew.

Lady Diana—she reputedly loathed the nickname "Lady Di"—was educated at West Heath School near Sevenoaks in Kent, and at a finishing school in Switzerland. Shortly after leaving school, she helped run the Young England kindergarten in Pimlico, London, managing also to fit in cleaning and babysitting jobs for friends, the very picture of a young upper-class English girl.

She first met Charles in 1977, ironically when he was courting her elder sister, Lady Sarah. But romance only blossomed—at least as far as the press was concerned—in 1980, at Balmoral, the Queen's Scottish home, when the couple were spotted on the banks of the river Dee by a journalist.

It seemed almost too good to be true. Here at last was a perfect specimen of what was widely believed an extinct species: a beautiful, aristocratic young girl, modest and kind, polite and charming, and, most important of all, with no "past" to sully her record. It would be difficult to imagine a better combination of attributes for a future Queen of England. Moreover, she appeared on the scene at precisely the point when the whispers about Prince Charles not having settled down were beginning to become just a little bit more insistent. After all, he was 33, surely rather old still to be sowing his wild oats while the future of the British throne remained uncertain.

Diana, in short, was perfect, a fairy tale indeed. She was welcomed with open arms by the Royal Family and the rest of the world alike. Her wedding to Prince Charles in St. Paul's Cathedral in July 1981 aroused phenomenal interest. It is estimated that 800 million people saw the ceremony live. Her winsome charm, easy manner and friendliness, allied to her impeccable fashion sense, have ensured continuing interest in every aspect of her life.

But her royal career has not been an unremitting story of happy ever after, perhaps not surprising in view of the strains imposed by her overnight elevation from obscurity to superstardom. The constant media attentions she endures have occasionally taken a heavy toll. So much so that during her engagement to Prince Charles, when gangs of reporters and photographers dogged her every step and made her life a misery, the Queen was moved to summon the editors of Britain's national press to Buckingham Palace to "request" they leave her alone. Likewise, Charles and Diana took the unusual step of allowing two TV films to be made about them in an attempt to stem the spread of rumor and gossip—much of it absurd invention.

The Princess also suffered badly during her first pregnancy, with Prince William, afterwards losing so much weight that there were fears she may have been suffering from the slimmer's disease, *anorexia nervosa,* a condition which had affected her sister.

But the Princess adores her two sons, Prince William and Prince Harry. Appropriately, she takes a particular interest in the problems of children and is patron of several children's charities, Dr. Barnardo's among them. She has also undertaken a number of overseas trips with her husband, notably to Australia, New Zealand, and Canada. In the process, her self-assurance and poise have grown by leaps and bounds, the blushing bride giving way gracefully to the mature young woman of today. Her position as the Royal Family's unofficial—but unmistakable—fashion trend-setter has also helped define her role.

For relaxation, the Princess enjoys embroidery and gardening at her homes in Kensington Palace, London, and Highgrove in Gloucestershire. Ballet and early-morning swims in the Buckingham Palace pool help her stay trim for the exhausting and demanding daily round. The problem, of course, with being an international fashion megastar is that you have to look your very best all the time. Second best just won't do.

- *Title:* Her Royal Highness THE PRINCESS OF WALES.

- *Name:* Lady Diana Frances Spencer.

- *Form of Address:* Your Royal Highness.

- *Born:* July 1, 1961, at Park House, Sandringham, Norfolk.

- *Married:* July 29, 1981, at St. Paul's Cathedral.

- *Residences:* Kensington Palace, London; Highgrove, Tetbury, Gloucestershire; Tamarisk, St. Mary's, Isles of Scilly. *Family Home:* Althorp, Northampton.

- *Honors:* 9th Princess of Wales.

- *Principal Patronages:* president, Welsh Crafts Council, and Albany Community Center, Deptford, southeast London; patron, Welsh National Opera, Swansea Festival of Music and the Arts, Malcolm Sargent Cancer Fund for Children, Birthright, Pre-school Playgroups Association, and National Children's Orchestra.

- *Children:* HRH PRINCE WILLIAM OF WALES (William Arthur Philip Louis), born June 21, 1982.
  HRH PRINCE HENRY OF WALES (Henry Charles Albert David), born September 15, 1984 (known as Prince Harry).

- *Interests:* Fashion, children, fishing, skiing, music, ballet, and swimming.

The Duke of York

"He's the one with the Robert Redford good looks," Prince Charles once said of his younger brother Prince Andrew, the Duke of York. Certainly, he has enjoyed a reputation both as a handsome playboy, with a string of beautiful girlfriends, and as a dashing war hero following the Falklands conflict.

Andrew Albert Christian Edward was born on February 19, 1960. He spent his childhood years at Buckingham Palace under the tutelage of his governess, Mabel Anderson. He quickly developed a reputation as a boisterous, vigorous child—

Prince Philip once attended a movie premiere sporting a black eye following a bedtime boxing match with his son.

He was sent to Heatherdown Preparatory School in 1968, and then moved to Gordonstoun. He fared creditably in his academic work, but performed with greater success on the sports field, becoming captain of the school cricket team. He subsequently spent two terms at Lakefield College, Ontario, where he was introduced to the delights of canoeing through the Rockies and ice hockey.

Since childhood, the Duke has been fascinated by helicopters. It was no surprise when he signed up for a Navy career that held out the promise of becoming a helicopter pilot. After passing his professional exams at Dartmouth College, he joined the aircraft carrier *H.M.S. Hermes* for a short period of training. He started learning to fly full-time after he graduated from Dartmouth, being assigned to 820 Squadron in *H.M.S. Invincible,* in which he served during the Falklands conflict in 1982.

During the campaign he was co-pilot in a Sea King helicopter, flying anti-submarine sorties and helping in the rescue of survivors from the doomed supply ship *Atlantic Conveyor.* Like many other young officers, Prince Andrew returned from the Falklands a more mature, reflective individual.

Shortly afterwards, a much publicized romance with American starlet Koo Stark sealed his fun-loving reputation. His notoriety, if not his popularity, was further fuelled when he sprayed a group of American photographers with paint during a visit to a Los Angeles housing development on his first foreign tour.

When not hitting the headlines, his abiding interest is photography. His first book, *Photographs,* received favorable reviews, although selling only moderately. Ever the enthusiast, he resorted to using his bathroom at Buckingham Palace as a darkroom.

He has continued to make a success of his chosen career. The Duke is a solid, capable Royal Navy lieutenant. It is expected that he will be promoted to lieutenant commander during his current two-year stint at Portland naval base in Dorset, where he is second in command of the weapons training school.

During his spell at Portland, the Duke and his wife, the former Miss Sarah Ferguson, are renting a large manor house called Chideock Manor near Bridport, Dorset, although the Queen is said to be ready to buy the couple their own home as a wedding gift once they find a suitable property.

- **Title:** His Royal Highness THE DUKE OF YORK, Earl of Inverness and Baron Killyleagh.

- **Name:** Andrew Albert Christian Edward.

- **Form of Address:** Your Royal Highness.

- **Born:** February 19, 1960, at Buckingham Palace.

- **Married:** July 23, 1986, at Westminster Abbey.

- **Residence:** Buckingham Palace, London.

- **Principal Patronages:** patron, British Schools Exploring Society, *SS Great Britain* Appeal, Jubilee Sailing Trust, and Aycliffe School; governor of Gordonstoun School.

- **Interests:** Flying, canoeing, exploring, and photography.

The Duchess of York

The Duchess of York, formerly Miss Sarah Ferguson—or "Fergie" to the world at large—is the latest addition to the fast growing Royal Family. Already she has become a popular figure, with her straightforward manner and obvious willingness to learn the royal routine. She is the second daughter of Major Ronald Ferguson, polo manager to Prince Charles, and Mrs. Susan Barrantes, now married to an Argentinian polo player, and author of the immortal utterance, when asked where her daughter and Prince Andrew had met, "On the polo field. Doesn't everyone?"

Sarah Margaret Ferguson was born in London on October 15, 1959. Although a commoner, she can trace her ancestry back to King Charles II and Robert the Bruce of Scotland. Through her paternal grandmother, Lady Elmhirst, a member of the family of the duke of Buccleuch, she has links with the Royal House of Stuart. Her grandmother is also a cousin of Princess Alice, dowager Duchess of Gloucester and the Queen's aunt through marriage.

Sarah spent her early years at her parents' home in Sunninghill, near Ascot in Berkshire. She was educated at two local boarding schools, Daneshill and Hurst Lodge, at the latter becoming joint head girl. But horseback riding and skiing took precedence over academic work, and she remains proficient in both sports.

On leaving school she attended a secretarial college in London before working in a public relations firm and an art gallery.

31

Since 1982 she has worked full-time for the London office of a Swiss-based printing company, commissioning authors and researching archival material for high-quality art books. She has continued her career since her marriage, and, commendably, intends to do so for the foreseeable future, at the same time fulfilling an increasing number of royal duties.

She has also become the first royal lady to win a private pilot's license, earning her wings in part so that she could understand better and share in her husband's career as a Navy flier. Characteristically, she has subsequently set her sights on learning to fly a helicopter.

- *Title:* Her Royal Highness THE DUCHESS OF YORK.

- *Name:* Sarah Margaret Ferguson.

- *Form of Address:* Your Royal Highness.

- *Born:* October 15, 1959, at the Welbeck Clinic, Marylebone, London.

- *Married:* July 23, 1986, at Westminster Abbey.

- *Residences:* Buckingham Palace. *Family Home:* Dummer Down Farm, near Basingstoke, Hampshire.

- *Interests:* Riding, tennis, and skiing.

Prince Edward

The Queen's youngest son has the reputation of being the most scholarly, quiet, and unassuming of her children. He was born in 1964 and given as his middle names Antony, after Lord Snowdon his uncle; Richard, after his cousin the Duke of Gloucester; and Louis, after Prince Philip's great-grandfather, Louis of Hesse.

He followed much the same educational path as Prince Andrew, attending Heatherdown Preparatory School before in 1977, going to Gordonstoun School, where, like Prince Charles before him, he became head boy. The Prince took part with enthusiasm in a number of outdoor pursuits, including skiing, rugby, sailing, riding, and shooting.

In 1983 he was admitted to Jesus College, Cambridge, where he studied history, graduating in 1986. During his three years at Cambridge he was a familiar figure, riding around the city streets on a bicycle, dutifully followed by his private detective. He had few privileges, and even took his weekly washing to the local laundromat. It was at Cambridge that his interest and ability in drama came to the fore. He appeared in a college production of Arthur Miller's *The Crucible* and several satirical revues.

Following Cambridge, his career seemed assured when he signed on with the Royal Marines as a cadet, or trainee, officer. Despite the Marines' well-earned reputation for toughness— their working motto is "First In, Last Out"—and the consequent trepidation with which many approach the course, Prince Philip was particularly pleased with his son's choice, being honorary captain general of the elite fighting force. However, after just four months' training at his Devon military camp, the Prince decided, amid a predictable blaze of publicity, that military life was not for him and resigned. It was a decision that many thought at least as tough to take as the course itself.

Since resigning his commission, Edward has found himself confronted with something of a dilemma as regards his career. Having spent two terms as a teacher in a New Zealand school before going to Cambridge, he has been slated as a future teacher, actor, and even, improbable as it sounds, TV announcer.

- *Title:* His Royal Highness THE PRINCE EDWARD.

- *Name:* Edward Antony Richard Louis.

- *Form of Address:* Your Royal Highness.

- *Born:* March 10, 1964, at Buckingham Palace.

- *Interests:* Rugby, drama, riding, and skiing.

The Princess Royal

The Queen's only daughter has today earned a well-deserved reputation as the hardest-working member of the Royal Family. As president of the Save the Children Fund, she has traveled to some of the most remote and impoverished regions of the Middle East, Africa, and India. This unstinting service on behalf of the world's deprived children has led to a startling change in her public image. Indeed, in 1985 she was voted Woman of the Year by a leading B.B.C. current affairs program, unlikely partner to Man of the Year Bob Geldof. In May 1987 her new-found popularity and esteem were further confirmed when the Queen granted her the title of Princess Royal. It was a signal honor, as the monarch's eldest daughter alone may be granted the title, and she holds it for life. It is, however, by no means automatically bestowed; it must, so to speak, be earned. Few today would deny that Princess Anne is anything but a worthy holder of the title.

It all makes an unlikely contrast to her early days. For years the "petulant Princess" was best known for roundly abusing the press, a habit she has never entirely lost. Her aloof, positively contemptuous manner led one American commentator to write, following a visit by the Princess to Washington, "Why not limit Princess Anne to opening rhododendron shows in Kent before unleashing her again on foreigners?"

Princess Anne was born at Clarence House on August 15, 1950. She received her early formal education at Buckingham Palace before spending a short time in France. She then attended Benenden, a girls' boarding school in Kent.

While she undertook several public duties as a teenager, her passion remained competitive horseback riding, especially three-day eventing, a gruelling all-round test of horse and rider, combining dressage, cross-country, and show jumping. In 1971 she won the Raleigh Trophy in the Individual European Three-Day Event at Burghley, Linconshire, an achievement that led to her being voted B.B.C.-TV's Sport's Personality of the Year. Her equestrian successes continued apace, culminating in 1976 when she won a place on the British team for the Montreal Olympics. Her Olympic debut was less than a triumph; she was thrown at one fence and received a slight concussion. But her critics were silenced by her gutsy and determined performance.

While she no longer rides at the highest competitive level, the Princess takes an active interest in the charity Riding for the Disabled. She is also president of the British Olympic Association.

Attacks on Princess Anne for her occasional tactlessness and refusal to compromise have tailed off significantly in recent years. What was once seen as gracelessness is now conceded to be the tough outer skin of a formidable personality. At the same time, her good works—very different from opening flower shows—have won her nothing but praise. Yet something of the old reputation remains, as the Princess herself acknowledges. "When I appear in public people expect me to neigh, grind my teeth, paw the ground, and swish my tail," she once tartly remarked.

In 1973 she married Captain Mark Phillips, a commoner, at

Westminister Abbey. Their marriage has been characterized by the earnest desire of both partners to distinguish between their public and their private lives. Captain Phillips, for example, always refers to his wife as "Princess Anne." This has not stopped the Princess from appearing on a number of TV talk shows, where she has displayed a dry and piercing wit.

But it's true also that this deliberately retiring posture may owe something to an attempted kidnapping of the Princess in March 1974. Then, an armed man fired several shots at her car as she drove down the Mall. The attempt was foiled, thanks largely to the bravery of her detective, James Beaton, who was himself wounded.

- **Title:** Her Royal Highness THE PRINCESS ROYAL.

- **Name:** Anne Elizabeth Alice Louise.

- **Form of Address:** Your Royal Highness.

- **Born:** August 15, 1950, at Clarence House, London.

- **Married:** November 14, 1973, at Westminster Abbey.

- **Residence:** Gatcombe Park, Minchinhampton, Gloucestershire.

- **Principal Patronages:** Chancellor, London University; president, Save The Children Fund, Overseas Mission to Seamen, British Academy of Film and Television Arts, Women's Royal Naval Service Benevolent Trust, British Olympic Association, and Chartered Institute of Transport; patron, Riding for the Disabled Association, Association of the Women's Royal Naval Service, Army and Royal Artillery Hunter Trials, British School of Osteopathy, Spinal Injuries Association, and National Union of Townswomen's Guilds; chief commandant, Women's Royal Naval Service, and St. John Ambulance Brigade Cadets.

- **Children:** Peter Mark Andrew Phillips, born November 15, 1977. Zara Anne Elizabeth Phillips, born May 15, 1981.

- **Interests:** Equestrianism and theater.

Mark Phillips

Mark Phillips is the son of a wealthy farmer turned businessman, Mr. Peter Phillips. He was educated at Stouts Hill Preparatory School and Marlborough School before joining the Army in 1967. After a two-year officers' course at the Royal Military Academy, Sandhurst, he was commissioned into the Queen's Dragoon Guards, becoming a troop leader with his regiment in

Hohne, West Germany. He was promoted to captain in 1973, and appointed a personal aide-de-camp to the Queen the following year after his marriage to Princess Anne.

While he had an undistinguished military career, Captain Phillips is nonetheless a world-renowned horseman, having been at varying times a European, World, and Olympic gold medallist. He has represented Britain at virtually every level, and has won a total of twelve three-day events. Additionally, he is the only man to have won the prized Badminton championship four times. Naturally, he and Princess Anne met through their mutual interest in horses; both have been riding since childhood.

After the couple's marriage at Westminister Abbey, watched by a television audience of more than 500 million, Captain Phillips quickly and deliberately faded out of the royal spotlight. At the beginning of his married life he said his dream was " that we may be allowed to have a private life." The principle has been steadfastly adhered to. While Princess Anne is a tireless royal worker, Captain Phillips is primarily a farmer, managing the couple's 1,200-acre estate in Gloucestershire, Gatcombe Park. The estate, a wedding gift from the Queen, is now also the site of an annual three-day horse trials organized by the captain.

Along with his farming interests, the captain—called Fog by his royal relations for being supposedly "thick and wet"—also comments on horse jumping for TV as well as spending several months of the year in Australia, where he conducts horse-riding clinics.

Captain Phillips has consistently refused to accept a royal title, stoutly mainting his status as a commoner. This has helped the royal couple bring up their children, Zara and Peter Phillips, in relative and welcome obscurity. Both children began their education at a local state-funded primary school in Minchinhampton near Gatcombe Park. Following more normal royal precedent, they have since moved on to private schools (these are called public schools in the U.S.).

- *Name:* Captain Mark Anthony Peter Phillips.

- *Form of Address:* Captain Phillips.

- *Born:* September 22, 1948, at Tetbury, Gloucestershire.

- *Married:* November 14, 1973, at Westminster Abbey.

- *Residence:* Gatcombe Park, Minchinhampton, Gloucestershire.
- *Honors:* Commander, Royal Victorian Order; personal A.D.C. to the Queen.
- *Interests:* Equestrianism.

The Queen Mother

Her Majesty Queen Elizabeth the Queen Mother—"the Queen Mum" to millions—personifies the charm and concern for her fellow man that characterize the Royal Family. "Duty is the rent we pay for living," she is fond of saying.

She was born Lady Elizabeth Angela Marguerite Bowes-Lyon on August 4, 1900, in London, the ninth of ten children of the Earl and Countess of Strathmore. Though not of royal blood, the family of Bowes-Lyon is descended from the royal houses of Scotland, while the venerable earldom of Strathmore dates from 1606.

Lady Elizabeth spent her early childhood at St. Paul's Waldenbury, her family's Hertfordshire home. Educated at home, she enjoyed a relaxed and happy childhood. During World War I, the family seat in Scotland, Glamis Castle, became a military hospital, and there the young Lady Elizabeth helped nurse men wounded in the fighting.

Her father was close to the Royal Family, and his children had known the children of the then King and Queen—George V and frosty, formidable Queen Mary—for many years. It was no surprise that the hand of vivacious and pretty Elizabeth was sought by the King's shy second son, the Duke of York. Characteristically, she turned him down, reluctant to give up her freedom for the stifling protocol of court life under George V. But the Duke persisted, and the couple were eventually married on April 26, 1923, at Westminister Abbey.

The new Duchess of York introduced a lighter note to royal life, quickly becoming popular as the "Smiling Duchess," and even winning the heart of starchy George V. When she was late for dinner, the King, a stickler for punctuality—he had all the clocks in the royal households set half an hour early—would brush aside her apologies with the words, "It was not you who was late, my dear. We must have sat down early" (as undoubtedly they had).

While she excludes an unmistakable and winning air of dignity and natural warmth, she possesses a thread of steel in her character. It's a quality that has proved invaluable on many occasions, notably during the abdication crisis of 1936 and, as Queen, during World War II.

Edward VIII's unprecedented decision to renounce his throne to marry American divorcee Wallis Simpson brought his brother, the Duke of York, dramatically to the throne. It was a position for which he was quite unsuited, both by training and by temperament, made all the more daunting by a stammer and frequent ill-health. The new King had, it is true, in striking contrast to his elder brother, inherited his father's strong sense of obligation and duty. But it is doubtful whether he could have coped with the stresses of both the abdication—the most serious crisis to afflict the Royal Family in modern times—and, just a few years later, the war, without the ever-present aid and comfort of his wife, "the most wonderful person in the world," in his touching phrase.

The war in fact brought out the very best qualities of King and Queen. Indeed, when Buckingham Palace was bombed she was, perversely it might seem, delighted. "Now we can look the East End in the face," she declared, referring to the slum district that had borne the brunt of the bombing. Both she and the King made frequent visits to scenes of destruction, helping to boost flagging morale.

George VI, racked with cancer and weakened by his untiring war work, died at Sandringham on February 6, 1952, aged only 56. For a time, the widowed Queen, given the courtesy title Queen Elizabeth the Queen Mother, considered bowing out of public life altogether. But her daughters would not hear of it (nor would Prime Minister Winston Churchill). She was persuaded to continue actively in public life.

Today she undertakes about 150 engagements a year, and has visited a number of foreign countries, including America, Canada, and Australia. Away from the public spotlight, which, it should be said, she steals most gracefully, she enjoys steeplechasing and salmon fishing—a sport she has practiced since childhood. She has had over 340 winners in 35 years of racing, although her greatest disappointment was to watch her horse Devon Loch lead the 1956 Grand National only to collapse dramatically and mysteriously just yards from the finishing post, an incident that even today she refuses to discuss.

While she has suffered a number of illnesses, particularly leg ulcers, the Queen Mother continues in robust good health, helped no doubt by the daily glass of champagne she has with her evening meal.

- **Title:** Her Majesty Queen Elizabeth THE QUEEN MOTHER.

- **Name:** Lady Elizabeth Angela Marguerite Bowes-Lyon.

- **Form of Address:** Your Majesty.

- **Born:** August 4, 1900, at 21 St. James's Square, London.

- **Married:** April 26, 1923, at Westminster Abbey (widowed February 6, 1952).

- **Residences:** Clarence House, London; The Royal Lodge, Windsor; Birkhall, Balmoral, Aberdeenshire, Scotland; Castle of Mey, Caithness, Scotland.

- **Honors:** Lady of the Garter; Lady of the Thistle; Dame Grand Cross, Royal Victorian Order, Order of the British Empire, and Order of St. John of Jerusalem.

- **Principal Patronages:** Lord Warden and Admiral of the Cinque Ports; Constable of Dover Castle; Chancellor, Dundee University; Fellow of the Royal Society; Commandant-in-Chief, R.A.F. Central Flying School; president, Royal College of Music; Master of the Bench, Middle Temple.

- **Children:** Her Majesty the QUEEN ELIZABETH Alexandra Mary, born April 21, 1926.
  HRH PRINCESS MARGARET Rose, born August 21, 1930.

- **Interests:** Horse racing, bloodstock breeding, fishing, and gardening.

Princess Margaret

"I can think of nothing more marvelous than being a Princess," Princess Margaret was once quoted as saying. It's an apt remark from the member of the Royal Family most generally associated in the public mind with the glamour of royalty, spiced with just the faintest whiff of scandal. Indeed, despite the promise of her early years, the title, "the Tragic Princess," coined many years ago, is not wholly inappropriate: Her life has been dogged by illness, thwarted love, and a marriage that turned sadly sour.

Princess Margaret Rose, the second and last child of King George VI and Queen Elizabeth, was born in 1930 at Glamis Castle, the Scottish home of her grandparents, the Earl and Countess of Strathmore. She was such a tiny baby that her sister nicknamed her "Bud."

Like her elder sister, she was educated in a Buckingham

Palace schoolroom. It was a rare treat when the two girls were allowed out with their governess to visit local parks or the London Zoo. She took part in her first great occasion of state, the coronation of her parents, in 1936 when she was just six.

The young Princess took up royal duties at an early age, focusing particularly on the Girl Guides. But it didn't take her long to discover that cafe society was much more fun than Girl Guiding. Indeed, she rapidly cultivated an image of daring, almost of rebellion. Smoking cigarettes in public was considerably more to her taste than putting up tents. She added an unmistakable sense of fun and style to the years of austerity following World War II.

Flaunting convention was one thing, but there was a point beyond which even the most headstrong young Princess ventured at her peril. Her desire to marry a dashing wartime pilot, Group Captain Peter Townsend, equerry to the King, was one such. Townsend, whatever his many other desirable qualifications, had one overriding drawback: He was divorced. To marry him, the Princess was obliged to obtain permission from the King and Queen. It was refused. The memory of Edward VIII's infatuation with a divorcee was too fresh to permit the possibility of future royal association with the divorce courts.

The episode caused lasting dismay to the couple, and additionally won the Princess a considerable measure of public sympathy. Thus was "the Tragic Princess" born.

But in 1960 Princess Margaret did marry, to society photographer Antony Armstrong-Jones. Once more, glamour and chic were introduced to the Royal Family. One could never accuse the Queen of being at the whim of fashion, plaything of the couturiers, but her sister and new husband introduced a dash of color, a touch of the Swinging Sixties, to the royal circle.

Eighteen years later, in a fanfare of newspaper headlines, the couple divorced. It was a step that would have been wholly unthinkable a generation earlier. The separation was amicable. Her former husband lives just half a mile from her Kensington Palace home, and often calls in to see her.

In tandem with her marriage troubles, the Princess drinks and smokes regularly and has suffered a series of illnesses. The most serious was in 1985 when she had an exploratory operation to test for lung cancer. It proved a false alarm.

Among her many interests are her home on the Caribbean island of Mustique, where both she and members of her family spend much time, and the theater and ballet. She is herself an accomplished pianist and singer. American musicals are her favorite, and she will regularly regale dinner guests until the small hours by singing the score from *Guys and Dolls* from memory.

While in recent years her life has not always been happy, she has nonetheless achieved a serenity and sang-froid, qualities reflected in the enthusiastic way she carries out a wide number of public engagements. She is a keen gardener, swims regularly, and in her youth was a fine horsewoman.

- *Title:* Her Royal Highness THE PRINCESS MARGARET.

- *Name:* Margaret Rose.

- *Form of Address:* Your Royal Highness.

- *Born:* August 21, 1930, at Glamis Castle, Tayside, Scotland.

- *Married:* May 6, 1960, Westminster Abbey (dissolved May 1978).

- *Residences:* Kensington Palace, London; Les Jolies Eaux, Mustique.

- *Honors:* Dame Grand Cross, Royal Victorian Order, and Order of St. John of Jerusalem; Honorary Doctor of Music, London University; Honorary Doctor of Letters, Keele University.

- *Principal Patronages:* Chancellor, Keele University; Master of the Bench, Lincoln's Inn; Colonel-in-Chief, Queen Alexandra's Royal Army Nursing Corps; vice-president, St. John's Ambulance Brigade.

- *Children:* David Albert Charles Armstrong-Jones, Viscount Linley, born November 3, 1961.
  Lady Sarah Frances Elizabeth Armstrong-Jones, born May 1, 1964.

- *Interests:* Music, theater, and ballet.

The Earl of Snowdon

Antony Armstrong-Jones was a veritable symbol of the Swinging Sixties. He was the first commoner to marry into the very center of the Royal Family (he was created the Earl of Snowdon just weeks before the birth of his first child, Viscount Linley), and his wedding to Princess Margaret in 1960 seemed to herald the dawn of a new age of openness and freshness in the royal ranks. The new royal couple were seen as the British equivalent of the Kennedys, exuding a vibrant charisma and vitality.

Yet in spite of his royal commitments, he continued his career as a photographer, a career that he has pursued with notable success to the present. Additionally, Lord Snowdon also designed a startlingly dramatic aviary for the London Zoo, and a revolutionary car for the handicapped. He also masterminded the Investiture of the Prince of Wales in 1969 at Caernarfon Castle, a successful and deeply imaginative ceremony.

While he accompanied Princess Margaret on many public engagements at home and abroad, he continually fought against the restrictions of royal life. "I am not a royal, I am just married to one," was his constant refrain.

Their marriage went adrift long before their divorce in 1978. Indeed for some years before then they had been living largely separate lives.

Lord Snowdon's and Princess Margaret's children, Viscount Linley and Lady Sarah Armstrong-Jones, have inherited their parents' artistic inclinations. Viscount Linley in particular shares his father's irreverent approach to life. For a bet he once arrived at a theater dressed in just a raincoat and rubber boots. He has also established a successful furniture-making business with two friends, selling their work from his shop—called, simply, David Linley—on Chelsea's King's Road.

His sister, Lady Sarah, has a similar artistic streak, studying textiles and designs at Camberwell Art College. She is very close to both parents and to the Princess of Wales, whom she often visits at her Kensington Palace apartments.

- *Title:* The Right Honourable THE EARL OF SNOWDON.

- *Name:* Antony Charles Robert Armstrong-Jones.

- *Form of Address:* My Lord.

- *Born:* March 7, 1930, in London.

- *Married:* 1) Princess Margaret, May 6, 1960, at Westminster Abbey (dissolved May 1978).

   2) Mrs. Lucy Lindsay-Hogg (Lucy Davies), December 15, 1978, at Kensington Register Office.

- *Honors:* Knight Grand Cross, Royal Victorian Order; Constable, Caernarfon Castle.

The Gloucesters

Richard, the Duke of Gloucester, grandson of George V and the Queen's first cousin, was destined for a quiet life as an architect when, in 1972, tragedy struck. His elder brother, William, a career civil servant, was killed in an air crash. Thus it was that two years later, on the death of his father, Richard became the new Duke of Gloucester.

After a childhood spent mainly in Australia, where his father was Governor General, Richard went to Magdelen College, Cambridge. It was on only his second day at Cambridge that he met Brigitte van Deurs, a Danish secretary, whom he married in July 1972.

On graduation, the future Duke—known as Proggie by his friends after his initials, PROG, standing for Prince Richard of Gloucester—set up as an architect with two colleagues. His life was ostensibly commonplace. Even his business cards, showing him as plain Richard Gloucester, gave nothing away.

But family tragedy in the shape of his brother's death in 1972, followed by that of his father in 1974, forced the young Duke to give up his career and assume a full-time royal role. Today, he and the Duchess perform around three public engagements a week, reserving weekends for their 2,500-acre farm at Barnwell Manor, Northamptonshire, near London.

The couple live simply, with the Duke spending much spare time on his hobbies of model making and photography. They are vociferously anti-smoking. They have three children—the Earl of Ulster, Lady Davina, and Lady Rose—with whom the Duke and Duchess spend as much of their time as possible.

Talented but unassuming, the Duke has been known to chafe at the restrictions of royal life. "Royalty must be professional ignoramuses," he complains. "It's a shame."

The Duke's mother, Princess Alice, still lives at Barnwell, though she sometimes spends the week with her family in that royal ghetto, Kensington Palace. Although well into her eighties, she still performs many public duties, especially for women's military and nursing organizations, both of which she was closely involved with during World War II.

The Duke of Gloucester

- *Title:* His Royal Highness THE DUKE OF GLOUCESTER.

- *Name:* Richard Alexander Walter George Windsor.

- *Form of Address:* Your Royal Highness.

- *Born:* August 26, 1944, in Northampton.

- *Married:* July 8, 1972, at Barnwell, Northamptonshire.

- *Residences:* Kensington Palace, London; Barnwell, Northamptonshire.

- **Honors:** Knight Grand Cross, Royal Victorian Order.

- **Principal Patronages:** Patron, Society of Engineers, Pestalozzi Children's Village Trust, Homeopathic Research Foundation Trust, and Council of Education in World Citizenship; president, Cancer Research Campaign, Institute of Advanced Motorists, National Association of Boys' Clubs, Christ's and St. Bartholomew's Hospitals, British Association of Dairy Farmers, British Consultants' Bureau, and U.K. National Committee of the International Council on Monuments and Sites; deputy chairman, Historic Buildings and Monuments Commission for England.

- **Interests:** Architecture, conservation, and photography. Both the Duke and Duchess enjoy skiing.

The Duchess of Gloucester
- **Title:** Her Royal Highness THE DUCHESS OF GLOUCESTER.

- **Name:** Brigitte Eva van Deurs

- **Form of Address:** Your Royal Highness.

- **Born:** June 20, 1946, in Odense, Denmark.

- **Children:** Alexander Patrick Gregers Richard Windsor, Earl of Ulster, born October 24, 1974.
   Lady Davina Elizabeth Alice Benedikte Windsor, born November 19, 1977.
   Lady Rose Victoria Brigitte Louise Windsor, born March 1, 1980.

Princess Alice
- **Title:** Her Royal Highness PRINCESS ALICE, Duchess of Gloucester.

- **Name:** Alice Christabel Montagu-Douglas-Scott.

- **Form of Address:** Your Royal Highness.

- **Born:** December 25, 1901, in London.

- **Married:** November 6, 1935, at Buckingham Palace.

- **Children:** Prince William of Gloucester (William Andrew Frederik) born December 18, 1941 (died August 28, 1972).
   Prince Richard (Richard Alexander Walter George) THE DUKE OF GLOUCESTER, born August 26, 1944.

The Kents

The Duke of Kent is one of the most able and versatile members of the Royal Family. At school he enjoyed rowing, in the Army he captained his regimental ski team. He is also a keen and capable horseman. As if this were not enough, the Duke, an enthusiastic photographer, also holds a pilot's license, is president of the All-England Lawn Tennis Club, and is an opera lover. Yet he had an unhappy time at school, where, as young Edward, he was shy and diffident and suffered from severe sinus trouble.

Edward, Duke of Kent, the eldest son of Princess Marina and grandson of George V—his father was George V's youngest son—was born in 1935. He was educated at Eton and Le Rosey, Switzerland, before entering the Royal Military College, Sandhurst, the first step to becoming a career soldier. He served with the Royal Scots Greys, retiring in 1976 with the rank of lieutenant colonel. Since leaving military life, he has spent much time as vice-chairman of the British Overseas Trade Board, banging the drum for British exports on frequent visits overseas.

In 1961 he married Katherine Worsley, daughter of Sir William Worsley, the former Lord Lieutenant of Yorkshire. She is a strikingly elegant woman, her sense of style admired by many, including Princess Margaret. Her work on behalf of the hospice movement and for children's charities has earned her a well-deserved place in the public's affections. Besides being an accomplished pianist, the Duchess regularly sings in a Bach choir.

Their only daughter, Lady Helen Windsor, has inherited her mother's talent for singing but not for public life. Like many young royals, she prefers to make her own career, and works for Christie's, the art auctioneers. Her youthful good looks and appearances at fashionable discos and parties have made her a regular in the Fleet Street gossip columns. Her brother, the Earl of St. Andrews, has shunned the public eye almost completely. He has recently finished a three-year history degree at Cambridge. In June 1987 his engagement to Canadian-born Sylvana Tomaselli was announced. The Kent's youngest child, Lord Nicholas Windsor, is still at school.

The Duke of Kent

- *Title:* His Royal Highness THE DUKE OF KENT.

- *Name:* Edward George Nicholas Paul Patrick Windsor.

- *Form of Address:* Your Royal Highness.

- *Born:* October 19, 1935, at 3 Belgrave Square, London.

- *Married:* June 8, 1961, at York Minster.

- *Residences:* York House, St. James's Palace, London; Anmer Hall, King's Lynn, Norfolk.

- **Honors:** Knight Grand Cross, Order of St. Michael and St. George, and Royal Victorian Order; personal A.D.C. to the Queen.

- **Principal Patronages:** Chancellor, Surrey University; Grand Master, United Grand (Freemasons') Lodge of England; president, Royal Institution, Royal National Lifeboat Institution, Commonwealth War Graves Commission, Royal United Services Institute, and All-England Lawn Tennis and Croquet Club (Wimbledon); patron, Kent Opera; vice-chairman, British Overseas Trade Board; non-executive director, British Insulated Callenders Cables.

- **Interests:** Skiing, riding, flying, opera, and photography.

The Duchess of Kent

- **Title:** Her Royal Highness THE DUCHESS OF KENT.

- **Name:** Katherine Lucy Mary Worsley.

- **Form of Address:** Your Royal Highness.

- **Born:** February 22, 1933, in Yorkshire.

- **Principal Patronages:** Chancellor, Leeds University; Controller Commandant, Women's Royal Army Corps; Colonel-in-Chief, Army Catering Corps; patron, Age Concern, British Epilepsy Association, The Samaritans, and Spastics Society.

- **Children:** George Philip Nicholas, Earl of St. Andrews, born June 26, 1962.
  Lady Helen Marina Lucy Windsor, born April 28, 1964.
  Lord Nicholas Charles Edward Jonathan Windsor, born July 25, 1970.

The Ogilvys

Elegant, jovial, and witty, Princess Alexandra, the Honorable Mrs. Angus Ogilvy, is one of the most unstuffy members of the Royal Family. With her brothers, the Duke of Kent and Prince Michael of Kent, she shares the unusual distinction of being a cousin of both the Queen, through her father, and the Duke of Edinburgh, through her mother, Princess Marina. She was five years old in 1942 when her father, Prince George, the former Duke of Kent, was killed in a flying accident while on active service in the war.

The Princess and her brothers were brought up in relative austerity by their mother at the family home of Coppins in Buckinghamshire. She became the first British Princess to have a normal education, attending Heathfield School in Ascot and a finishing school in Paris, where she studied languages and music. She was pressed into royal service as soon as she reached maturity, and has continued to shoulder a busy round of public engagements ever since, frequently representing the Queen abroad. In 1986, for example, she visited Thailand, Hong Kong, and the United States.

Her marriage to the Honorable Angus Ogilvy took place with much pomp at Westminster Abbey in 1963. His family, of Scottish descent, has close associations with the Royal Family. Mr. Ogilvy, besides being the patron of a number of charities, including the Imperial Cancer Research Fund, is a City businessman and director of a number of organizations, including Sotheby's. Like so many other members of the Royal Family, he is also actively engaged in charity work.

Their eldest child, James Ogilvy, followed his father to Eton and is currently reading for an arts degree at St. Andrew's University in Scotland. Their daughter, Marina, showed her independence after finishing school when she won a place on Operation Raleigh, a scheme designed to send young people to Third World countries to help on vital projects. Neither child will take any part in royal life.

Princess Alexandra

- **Title:** Her Royal Highness PRINCESS ALEXANDRA, the Honorable Mrs. Angus Ogilvy.

- **Name:** Alexandra Helen Olga Christabel.

- **Form of Address:** Your Royal Highness.

- **Born:** December 25, 1936, at 3 Belgrave Square, London.

- **Married:** April 24, 1963, at Westminster Abbey.

- **Children:** James Robert Bruce Ogilvy, born February 29, 1964. Marina Victoria Alexandra Ogilvy, born July 31, 1966.

- **Residences:** Thatched House Lodge, Richmond; Friary Court, St. James's Palace, London.

- **Honors:** Dame Grand Cross, Royal Victorian Order.

- **Principal Patronages:** Vice-president, British Red Cross Society; chancellor, Lancaster University; patron, Princess Mary's Royal Air Force Nursing Service, Queen Alexandra's Royal Naval Nursing Service, and Guide Dogs for the Blind Association; president, Royal Commonwealth Society for the Blind, and Alexandra Rose Day; Honorary Commandant General, Royal Hong Kong Police Force.

- **Interests:** Music, skiing, riding, and swimming.

47

The Honorable Angus Ogilvy

- *Name:* The Honorable Angus James Bruce Ogilvy.

- *Form of Address:* Mr. Ogilvy.

- *Born:* September 14, 1928.

- *Principal Patronages:* Member, Royal Company of Archers of Scotland; president, British Rheumatism and Arthritis Association, Imperial Cancer Research Fund, National Association of Youth Clubs, and Scottish Wildlife Trust.

The Michaels of Kent

Flamboyant, controversial, and glamorous, Prince and Princess Michael of Kent have risen from relative obscurity to a fame—indeed a notoriety—almost rivaling that enjoyed by any other member of the Royal Family.

Before his marriage, Prince Michael, the third and youngest child of the late Duke and Duchess of Kent, born in 1942, was known as a military man and daredevil sportsman. The Prince, who earned the rank of major in the Royal Hussars, had a passion for dangerous winter sports. He represented the Army in the Inter-Services Bobsleigh Championships, becoming driver for the British team in the European Championships and winning the British Bobsleigh Championship at St. Moritz, Switzerland, in 1972. He did not survive entirely unscathed, suffering neck and chin injuries in a crash during practice for the World Four-Man Championship.

The Prince also enjoys the challenge of fast cars. He has driven in several international rallys, notably the 1970 London-to-Mexico World Cup Rally. In 1969 he also took part in the Daily Mail Transatlantic Air Race.

While something of a real-life Action Man, he was nonetheless little known to the general public until his marriage in 1978 to Baroness Marie-Christine von Reibnitz. Not only was the Czech-born baroness a practicing Catholic, she was also a divorcee. To marry her, Prince Michael had to obtain permission from the Queen, head of the Church of England. This was duly given, but at the same time the Prince was also obliged to renounce his (admittedly distant) claim to the throne.

While the marriage was blessed at a private ceremony by the Archbishop of Canterbury, it was not until 1983 that the Pope agreed to allow the couple to marry in the Catholic rite. However, both their children—Lord Frederick Windsor and Lady Gabriella Windsor—will be brought up as Protestants.

Princess Michael, blond, statuesque, and eternally effervescent, quickly captured the public's imagination. But since her marriage, she has demonstrated an unerring ability to hit the headlines for all the wrong reasons. Thus, considerable shock waves were caused by the revelation that her father had been a member of Hitler's feared SS. Shortly afterwards, her image was further dented when her secret friendship with Texas property tycoon John Ward Hunt was made public.

Since then, the Princess has been dogged by controversy. The publication of her first book—about the lives of Queens born in other countries—lead to charges of plagiarism. Meanwhile, a series of interviews she undertook to publicize the book added to the controversy. Notably, she admitted that she found charity work "boring," that the British loved failure, and that she wanted to live in America. None of which tended to endear her greatly to the British public, or indeed to other members of the Royal Family.

When she is not courting controversy, the Princess is a skilled interior decorator, specializing in restoring 18th-century houses. She also skis superbly, plays tennis regularly, has taken up eventing actively, and loves the company of friends.

While the royal couple do not receive any Civil List payment, Prince Michael holds a number of City directorships that help defray staff costs.

Prince Michael
- *Title:* His Royal Highness PRINCE MICHAEL OF KENT.

- *Name:* Michael George Charles Franklin.

- *Form of Address:* Your Royal Highness.

- *Born:* July 4, 1942, at Coppins, Iver, Buckinghamshire.

- *Married:* June 30, 1978, in the Rathaus, Vienna, Austria.

- *Residences:* Kensington Palace, London; Nether Lypiatt Manor, Gloucestershire.

- *Principal Patronages:* President, Royal Life Savings Society, Royal Automobile Club, Society of Genealogists, Institute of the Motor Industry, Motor Industry Research Association, the Sailors', Soldiers', and Airmens' Families Association, and Kennel Club; trustee, National Motor Museum; director, Standard Telephones and Cables, and Aitken Hume; vice-chairman, Walbrook Insurance Ltd.

49

- *Interests:* Flying, hunting, squash, and skiing.

Princess Michael

- *Title:* Her Royal Highness PRINCESS MICHAEL OF KENT.

- *Name:* Marie-Christine Anne Agnes Hedwig Ida von Reibnitz.

- *Form of Address:* Your Royal Highness.

- *Born:* January 15, 1945, in Karlsbad, Bohemia (now Czechoslovakia).

- *Married:* 1) Mr. Tom Troubridge, 1971 (dissolved in 1977).
     2) Prince Michael of Kent, June 30, 1978, in the Rathaus, Vienna, Austria.

- *Children:* Lord Frederick Michael George David Louis Windsor, born April 6, 1979.
     Lady Gabriella Marina Alexandra Ophelia Windsor, born April 23, 1981.

- *Principal Patronages:* Trustee, Victoria and Albert Museum; patron, British Ski Federation, Breast Cancer Research Trust, Society of Women Artists, Royal Shakespeare Theater Trust, and Arab Horse Society; president, Tufty Club (Royal Society for the Prevention of Accidents).

- *Interests:* Equestrianism, skiing, and writing.

- *Publication:* Crowned in a Far Country (1986).

THE ROYAL YEAR

Two American tourists were standing in line for hamburgers at an English country show. They looked at each other in disbelief. Ahead of them was a young mother holding the hand of a sandy-haired boy. It was Princess Anne and her son, Peter Phillips.

This cameo epitomizes so much of Britain's Royal Family. They are among the most famous faces in the world, yet they remain immensely accessible. Other than at the most formal occasions, the Queen and her family keep security down to a minimum. The round-the-clock security that surrounds the President of the United States is quite alien to them. They are there to be seen. Indeed, their accessibility is one of their greatest strengths.

Another is their predictability. Even at play, the members of the Royal Family have a routine you could practically set your watch by. Christmas at Windsor, New Year at Sandringham, Easter at Windsor, summer at Balmoral. Within this royal round are a host of formal and informal events that take place year-in, year-out with absolute reliability. Trooping the Color, Royal Ascot, Cowes, any one of a huge number of country horse trials, polo matches, the Derby, the State Opening of Parliament—the list is endless.

Our Royal Year sets out the whens and the wheres, all with full descriptions of who will be there and what's going on. Planning ahead is easy. But remember that, as well as these annual events, all the Royal Family perform a large number of engagements that vary year by year: visiting a hospital, opening a school, touring a factory, opening a museum, entertaining foreign dignitaries, and, of course, making trips overseas. None of these events is liable to be known long in advance. So, if you want to know which member of the Royal Family is doing what on any given day, look at the Court and Social pages of the British papers *The Times,* the *Daily Telegraph,* the *Independent,* or the *Star.* All four newspapers will give details. They'll also confirm details of the events we list here.

If you are at an event where there is the possibility of the Royal Family mingling with the crowd—and remember, Prince Charles and Princess Diana do this most frequently—bear in mind the following tips:

—Don't stand near the press photographers. The royals will *never* make for the side of the road where they are standing.

—Wear something bright or that will give the royal in question a topic of conservation. A silly hat, a club badge, or tie always gets them talking.

—If you want to give them flowers, make sure your gift is small.

—Stand as near as possible to the door or exit from which they will leave. During an unscheduled walkabout they won't stay too long.

Finally, we have graded all the occasions we list here from one to five crowns. Those with five mean that the event is either very spectacular or that there will be many members of the Royal Family present, and very often informally, of course. Those with one crown will be least spectacular or will have just one or two members of the family present.

JANUARY

Sandringham

 The first month of the year sees the members of the Royal Family on their official vacation at the Queen's country retreat of Sandringham in Norfolk. Here the entire family gathers to celebrate New Year in the turreted country manor house. They are a notoriously healthy bunch, and spend their days shooting, riding, and enjoying winter picnics on the beach at nearby Holkham or at their Scandinavian-style cabin on the 20,000-acre estate.

Even on holiday the Queen and her family have a routine which, if not virtually changeless, is the next best thing to it. At 9:30 sharp a stretch shooting wagon pulls out from the Jubilee Gates of the "Big House" with seven guns on board. Prince Philip normally leads the shooting party, though he is by no means the sharpest shot; Captain Mark Phillips, Princess Anne's husband, is said to have the keenest eye, with Prince Andrew and Prince Edward not far behind.

At around 9:30, too, keen royal watchers will gather near the stables 200 yards from the main house. Every morning the Queen, in her distinctive beige cape and scarf, spends an hour

Sandringham

or so in the saddle, often accompanied by her daughters-in-law, the Princess of Wales and the Duchess of York.

Don't get too close to either party, however, or you risk the rough edge of a royal tongue. Britain's royals guard their vacation privacy jealously, and not surprisingly resent sightseers clamoring to take photographs. Be this as it may, with a bit of luck and a hefty dose of discretion those onlookers who keep their distance are likely to be left alone.

If approaching the manor house seems too forward for your taste, you're bound to bump into a member of the Royal Family sooner or later if you walk about the muddy lanes near Sandringham and West Newton: the Duke of Kent taking a stroll with his daughter, Lady Helen Windsor, or the Queen herself, out walking her black Labrador dogs and the odd waddling corgi. If all else fails, there's a guaranteed opportunity of sighting the Queen, the Queen Mother, Princess Diana, and the other Royal Family members, at the Sandringham church services.

- **Dates:** Throughout January and the early part of February.

- **Venue:** Sandringham House, King's Lynn, Norfolk (tel. 0553–772675). See also "Sandringham" in the *Royal Residences* chapter.

- **Getting There:** *By Car*—From London take the M11 to exit 14 and then the A10 to King's Lynn. From there, take the A148 to Fakenham and then the B1440 to Sandringham.

Sandringham Church Service

Set within the grounds of the Sandringham estate, the picturesque 14th-century Church of St. Mary Magdalen is a charming backdrop for the Royal Family's first winter outings in public. Normally up to 10,000 patient well-wishers wait from the early hours for a glimpse of the family on their way to and from church. It always seems to be raining, and it is always cold; the routine is as predictable as the weather.

Early arrivals—especially families with children—are allowed into the church precincts to stand in roped-off sections. When the local police feel these are full to capacity they will only permit sightseers to stand by the roadside to watch the royal cars go by, so the first rule is to get there early—10:00 A.M. is late! Bring a thermos or hip flask, wrap up warmly, and to pass the time carry along the Sunday papers or simply chat to the locals who, despite their familiarity with the royal routine, never

The Queen's procession toward the House of Lords during the State Opening of Parliament.

Just a face in the crowd: the Queen of England in her natural habitat (top). Headscarf carefully knotted, the Queen walks with the Duke of York during Badminton Horse Trials

Prince Charles and his bride by the banks of the river Dee at Balmoral during their honeymoon.

Contrasting faces of the Queen: top, in the Irish State Coach on her way to the State Opening of Parliament; bottom, at the wheel of her Range Rover at the Royal Windsor Horse Trials.

Prince Philip demonstrates his considerable skill in the complex art of carriage driving on the grounds of Windsor Castle.

Away from madding crowds: Prince Charles fishing for salmon at Balmoral. Below, the royal yacht Britannia *on the Solent during Cowes Week.*

The Prince aims to get in at least one game a week during the summer.

SUNDAY MORNING AT SUNDRINGHAM

Princess Diana and Princess Anne with her daughter, Zara, head through the snow for home after church.

The Royal Family gather on the balcony of Buckingham Palace after the Trooping of the Color to watch the traditional flypast by the Royal Air Force.

The Queen Mother, Prince Charles, and Princess Diana in the less formal setting of the Braemar Games in Scotland.

The time-honored gathering outside Clarence House on the morning of the Queen Mother's birthday in August (top). The Queen Mother greets Prince Charles on a wet morning at Scrabster at the end of the Royal Family's annual summer Scottish cruise (bottom).

Prince Andrew and Sarah Ferguson before their marriage, waiting to present the trophies after a polo match at Windsor.

Princess Anne comes a cropper at the water jump at the Badminton Horse Trials (top). The Queen, secure in her saddle, at the Trooping of the Color (bottom).

Princess Anne in a reflective mood at the Badminton Horse Trials.

Princess Michael of Kent and a friend.

Princess Anne with children Zara and Peter Philips.

Top, Princess Margaret and the Queen Mother on the traditional drive down the course at Royal Ascot. Bottom, Lady Sarah Armstrong-Jones demonstrates a more informal way of getting around.

seem to get bored with it. For many the trip is seen as a jolly morning's outing, and picnic baskets are not unusual additions to the scene on those rare occasions when the weather is good.

Shortly before 11:00 the royal cars draw up, those of the Queen, the Queen Mother, Prince Philip, Prince Charles, and Princess Diana leading the way, while the Duke and Duchess of Kent and their children—Lady Helen Windsor, the Earl of St. Andrews, and Lord Nicholas Windsor—arrive separately from their nearby country manor, Anmer Hall. After greeting the vicar, family members walk slowly along the path to the church, giving photographers and sightseers ample opportunity to appreciate their Sunday finery.

The service, which can last up to ninety minutes, is relayed outside through loudspeakers, and the waiting crowd often joins in the hymns. A guest preacher is always brought in for the sermon. A former Speaker of the House of Commons, Lord Tonypandy, is a royal favorite. Family tradition dictates the preacher stay for the weekend at Sandringham House.

After the final hymns and prayers, the Royal Family leaves the church and gathers in the entrance archway to receive bunches of flowers from dozens of children; the Princess of Wales and the Duchess of York are the most popular recipients. When the children have presented their gifts, the men and younger ladies, including Princess Diana, walk back to the manor through the park, wishing a cheery "Good morning" on the way to sightseers no more than an arm's length from the royal party. The Queen and the Queen Mother, however, generally return by car.

As the month progresses, fewer and fewer younger royals attend church services, as they will have flown to various Alpine resorts for their annual skiing vacations.

- **Dates and Times:** Sunday mornings at 11:00 during the Royal Family's residence at Sandringham in January and early February.

- **Venue:** Church of St. Mary Magdalen, Sandringham, Norfolk.

- **Getting There:** See directions for Sandringham, above.

FEBRUARY

Until early February the Queen, Prince Philip, and the Queen Mother remain in residence at Sandringham. Princess Margaret normally journeys at this time to the tiny Caribbean island of Mustique, where she has her own cliff-top villa. But the holiday is over for Prince Charles and Princess Diana, who are back at work on their official engagements, as are Princess Anne, the Duke and Duchess of York, and Prince Edward.

The church service at Sandringham continues as described in January, but for serious royalty watchers, February is a month for sending in applications for Royal Ascot and the Garter Ceremony, both held in June.

Unfortunately, apart from the royal engagements announced in the Court and Social pages of *The Times,* the *Daily Telegraph,* the *Independent,* and the *Star,* February is a rather bleak month for royal sightings. The only sure chance is to stand outside the security barrier at Kensington Palace and watch the royal cars come and go; in an hour it is surprising whom you may see. Early in the morning you may spot Princess Diana going off for her morning swim at the Buckingham Palace pool, or Prince William being taken by a detective to school in nearby Notting Hill. The comings and goings of delivery vans and royal courtiers can also give a fascinating insight into the daily routine of the royal families who live within the red brick walls of Kensington Palace.

If you wish to savor the past, pay a visit to the palace's state apartments, which contain a superb exhibition of court costumes and memorabilia.

- *Venue:* Kensington Palace, Kensington Gardens, London W8.

- *Getting There:* *Tubes*—High Street Kensington, Notting Hill Gate, Queensway. See also "Kensington Palace" in the *Royal Residences* chapter.

MARCH

The members of the Royal Family are hard at work during March, their diaries filled with engagements both public and private. Throughout the month there are often various official state visits from overseas heads of state. In 1987, for instance,

King Fahd of Saudi Arabia made a five-day official visit. He was treated to the full majesty of monarchy, with open horse-drawn carriages and a glittering escort of the Horsehold Cavalry through the streets of London.

March also heralds the start of the equestrian eventing season (a combination of dressage, cross-country, and show-jumping events), giving the royal watcher an excellent opportunity to see the horse-mad members of the Royal Family enjoying themselves away from the pomp and protocol of their official duties. However, the most important event this month is essentially ecclesiastical in nature—the Royal Maundy.

The Royal Maundy

 On Maundy Thursday—or Holy Thursday—of each year, the Queen takes part in an ancient ritual by presenting alms to a group of worthy recipients whose number is determined by her current age (as is the number of coins in her donations). In 1987, for example, Queen Elizabeth was 61, so 61 men and 61 women received the purses, each containing 61 coins.

The ceremony, which dates from the twelfth century, symbolically commemorates Christ washing the apostles' feet at the Last Supper, on the eve of the Crucifixion. The coins are highly prized silver pennies to the value of one, two, three, and four "sterlings"—the original name for coins used in Norman times.

In addition to giving alms to the Christian poor, earlier monarchs would also wash their feet in a surprising act of humility—imagine, if you can, the vast bulk of Henry VIII lumbering down to perform this chore. Sometime in the seventeenth century this part of the ceremony was abandoned, though the Queen is nonetheless presented with sweet-smelling nosegays by children of the parish as a reminder of former duties, while a ceremonial officer known as the Lord High Almoner still symbolically girds himself with linen towels.

The men and women who receive the Maundy purses are carefully chosen on the recommendation of the clergy in the diocese to be visited. Three conditions must be met: the recipients must be over 65, Christian, and financially needy. During the service the men and women who receive the royal purses sit on opposite sides of the cathedral. The Queen then goes slowly down one side handing out purses to the women first, then turns back up the other side for the men.

- **Date and Time:** Thursday before Easter (anytime between mid-March and mid-April), generally starting at 11:00.

- **Venue:** Every fourth year in London's Westminster Abbey, other years in various cathedrals throughout the country.

- **Getting In:** Arrangements for the public to attend the Maundy service vary from year to year depending upon its location. Tickets are always needed, however, and you should contact the Dean and Chapter of the cathedral concerned. (The cathedral is selected the previous November; the best way to find out is to call Buckingham Palace at 930 4832). Most visitors are content to watch the procession of Queen, clergy, and recipients from outside the cathedral, for which no ticket is needed. On the day of the Maundy service the venue is announced in the Court and Social columns of *The Times,* the *Daily Telegraph,* the *Independent,* and the *Star.*

Crookham Horse Trials

The eagerly anticipated equestrian eventing season gets smoothly underway with the Crookham Trials. Princess Anne and her children, Zara and Peter Phillips, together with her husband, Captain Mark Phillips, are annual visitors—and very often competitors—at these events. If you're lucky you may also catch Princess Michael of Kent trying her hand at the novice hurdles. The blond princess took up three-day eventing (a day for each of the events—dressage, cross-country, and show-jumping) in her late thirties, and, although she does not lack courage, her tutors nonetheless fear the princess lacks the necessary equine skill. As a result, she has come a cropper at a number of the more difficult fences, though she takes her spills philosophically: "At least I land gracefully," she says with a rueful smile.

Princess Anne competes in a different league, however. If members of the Royal Family were simply known as the Windsors, Anne Windsor would be renowned throughout the world for her equine achievements. The stalwart Princess was a member of the British Olympic team in 1976 and European Three-Day Eventing Champion in 1971, though in recent years she has been plagued by unsuitable mounts. Her husband, the dashing Captain Mark Phillips, is also a world-class rider.

Informality is the keynote at these country horse shows. The Princess will wander around in her green rubber boots—*everyone* seems to have green boots at these affairs!—faded jeans, and a headscarf, knowledgeably searching for bargains among the many stalls which follow the horse trials on their annual circuit. Peter and Zara are often spotted racing freely among the crowds.

Once, a Cockney photographer, spotting Peter Phillips among the crowd, asked him, "Do you want to earn ten pence?" "Yes, please," replied Peter politely. "Then stand still for a minute," ordered the photographer. He took his pictures of the boy before casually flicking him the money.

Few visitors have the nerve to get away with this kind of stunt; nor is it very desirable. Princess Anne is very protective of her children, preferring them to lead lives as private as possible. She gets annoyed when photographed at what she considers private events. On one famous occasion she told a group of camera-men to "naff off" for snapping her picture just before she was to compete. The Princess pleads her case by saying she is nervous, her mount is frisky, and she must be allowed to con-centrate on the job in hand—clearing 18 or so fences without making a mistake.

The March weather is frequently cold and wet, so wrap up warmly. Take rubber boots and a good raincoat or waterproof jacket—a hip flask isn't a bad item to tote along, either! The golden rule at all informal royal events is to keep your eyes peeled, being discreetly aware of who is around you.

- *Dates and Times:* First weekend of the month.

- *Venue:* Tweseldown Racecourse, Fleet, Hampshire.

- *Getting There: By Car*—Exit 5 on the M3; take the A287 towards Church Crookham, then follow the blue-and-white RAC signs.

Barnsley Park Horse Trials

 A small country event, the Barnsley Park trials usually see about 50 horses and riders competing for cups and trophies. The royal presence is pro-vided in the form of Princess Michael of Kent, who has competed in the novice events, while a dutiful Prince Michael often travels from their nearby home of Nether Lypiatt to see his wife perform. The devout horse lovers Princess Anne and Captain Mark Phillips are, of course, regulars.

While this is a very small affair, it nonetheless affords a good opportunity to see the royals relaxing without the crowds and photographers who usually dog their heels. If you don't mind a little mud—well, a lot of mud, really—and are prepared to take a risk that the royals might not turn up, you could well see Princess Anne or one of the other members of the family in situations that never arise on official public engagements when everyone is on best behavior.

- **Date:** Second Saturday of the month.

- **Venue:** Barnsley Park, Cirencester, Gloucestershire.

- **Getting There:** *By Car*—Exit 15 from the M5 towards Cirencester on the A419; take the A433 to Barnsley and follow the blue-and-white RAC signs.

Cheltenham National Cup Festival Hunt Meeting

 Cheltenham is reputedly the Queen Mother's favorite racing festival. But it is one that also attracts serious horse-race enthusiasts from all corners of the world, especially Ireland. The best chasers and hurdlers come for a chance to win the coveted Cheltenham Gold Cup. Practiced royal watchers have the opportunity of seeing the Queen Mum having a whale of a time expertly eyeing up the prancing horseflesh (don't let her cuddly looks fool you; it's said the Queen Mother can spot a winner at 100 paces with one eye closed).

This is an informal, lively meeting, and the Queen Mother thoroughly enjoys chatting to racegoers about the sport's finer points—spavins, fetlocks, accumulators, and the like. While she has her own royal box from which to watch the day's progress, it is not at all unusual to find her making towards the paddock to examine the horses. And often members of the public have brushed past the lady in an emerald green coat only to realize too late they have inadvertently jostled the Queen Mother. One famous occasion was captured forever by television cameras: A gentleman racegoer was about to walk past her, realized who she was, and, in a terrible confusion, attempted to genuflect, bow, and raise his hat all at the same time.

The Queen Mother is always accompanied by her granddaughter, Princess Anne, and occasionally by the Prince and Princess of Wales.

- **Dates:** Between March 17 and 19 for three days.

- **Venue:** Cheltenham, Gloucestershire.

Cheltenham

- **Getting There:** *By Car*—Take the M40 from London, then the A40, to Oxford and Cheltenham; then follow the blue-and-white RAC signs.

APRIL

Spring is here at last: Cherry blossoms are in full bloom, swathes of nodding daffodils brighten many a village green, and the evocative crack of bat against cricket ball can again be heard. April heralds royal events, as well. Prince Charles's thoughts turn once more to the pleasures and perils of the polo field; crowds of well-wishers vie to glimpse the Queen and other members of the Royal Family at the Easter church services at Windsor; and the royals turn out en masse to enjoy the three-day Badminton Horse Trials.

Ermington Horse Trials

 Princess Anne and, very occasionally, Princess Michael of Kent will attend this small-scale horse show, which is held in the rolling hills of Devon. The cross-country course is set in undulating terrain with a short hill towards the finish, and includes several tough water obstacles. Though the royal element cannot always be counted on, this event can nonetheless afford an enjoyable and rewarding day's outing.

- *Date:* April 1.

- *Venue:* Flete, Ermington, Devon.

- *Getting There: By Car*—Take the A38 Exeter-Plymouth road, turn left at the Ivybridge signpost, then follow the road through to Ermington; the show is signposted from this point.

Easter at Windsor Castle

For the Queen, Easter marks the beginning of a six-week stay at Windsor Castle. At Easter itself all the immediate members of the family gather under one roof. The Queen Mother leaves her own nearby home—the Royal Lodge in Windsor Great Park—to stay with her daughter, but soon returns to the lodge for the remainder of the Easter break. On Good Friday, the Queen retreats to her own private chapel in the Brunswick Tower, and during the day the rest of the Royal Family arrive at the castle.

As the entire Court moves to Windsor for the long stay, so, too, does a small army of back-up staff. It's quite an exodus from Buckingham Palace: Equerries and ladies-in-waiting arrive in chauffeur-driven cars, busloads of housemaids roll up, mountains of luggage are shifted by soldiers in military trucks, and the Pipe Major comes along, too, who, when he is not piping under the Queen's castle bedroom window, doubles as the royal film projectionist (in the Royal Family's own movie theater). During the comings and goings the castle is open to the public, and visitors may be fortunate enough to catch a glimpse of Princess Diana or the royal children arriving in the castle precincts.

Around lunchtime on Easter Saturday the Queen will lead the Royal Family to the green drawing room on the second floor of the Queen's Tower, from where they will watch a military band playing a selection of melodies. Few members of the public realize the East Terrace is open to the public, and, as members of the Royal Family sit in the window appreciating the band, onlookers can often closely observe them before they disappear back into the depths of the castle.

On Easter Sunday, visitors can be assured of seeing the royals trooping off to St. George's Chapel to fulfill their Easter obligation. Unlike the Christmas services at Sandringham, the Easter gathering of the royal clan does not normally include the Gloucesters, the Michaels of Kent, the Kents, or the Ogilvys, though the format is similar. The public is allowed within the castle grounds to see the family go to the chapel, and promptly at 11:00 A.M. the 50-minute service begins. As with all royal events, though, members of the public should arrive in plenty of time to be assured of a good position. Visitors can see the Royal Family in their Easter finery both entering and leaving the chapel, when the Queen and other members of the family walk slowly back to their cars to enable even the clumsiest photographer to take a good snapshot. A truly thoughtful monarch, the Queen will often turn down the offer of an umbrella when it is raining to let the crowd have a better look at her face.

- **Dates:** Good Friday, Holy Saturday, and Easter Sunday.

- **Venue:** Windsor Castle, Windsor, Royal Berkshire (tel. 0753–868286). See also "Windsor Castle" in the *Royal Residences* chapter.

- **Getting There:** *By Car*—Take the M4 from London. *By Train*—from Waterloo Station every half hour; journey time approx. 50 minutes; tel. 928 5100 for train times and fares. *By Bus*—Three Greenline buses from Victoria Coach Station, Eccleston Bridge, London S.W.1; journey time approx. 60 minutes; tel. 834 6563 for times and fares.

Hagley Hall Horse Trials

 Princess Anne and Captain Mark Phillips, together with their children, Zara and Peter, will often appear at these cross-country trials. The event has the distinct advantage of being relatively crowd-free in comparison with Badminton and some of the other royal-watching excursions. An obvious rule of thumb is the less people present, the greater the chance you will actually find yourself next to your favorite royal.

- **Dates:** Easter Sunday and the following Monday.

- **Venue:** Hagley Hall, Stourbridge, West Midlands.

- **Getting There:** By Car—Hagley Hall, owned by Viscount Cobham, is four miles from the M5 (exits 4 or 5) on the A456 Kidderminister-Birmingham road; signposted approach roads.

Badminton Horse Trials

Founded in 1949 by the 10th Duke of Beaufort (on whose land the show takes place), the Badminton Horse Trials exudes the sort of cachet normally associated with top events in that time-honored tradition known by millions of *My Fair Lady* and Oscar Wilde fans as "The Season." Badminton today extends over four days and is the greatest and grandest equestrian event of its kind. In past years the Queen and other members of the Royal Family would traditionally stay at Badminton with their hosts (and distant relations) the Duke and Duchess of Beaufort, though the 10th Duke's death in 1984 put an end to this custom. This royal affair attracts huge crowds; these days nearly 300,000 spectators attend the four-day event, with the cross-country day seeing by far the biggest crush.

Top English show-jumper Lucinda Green, describing the thrill of the occasion, ascribes to it "an extraordinary atmosphere—both forbidding and friendly. It's a tremendously impressive place, this huge house in its own park, and for the competitors there's always an edge of apprehension and terror. For everyone else," she adds, "it's a lovely day out, a part of the country set's entertainment. Competing here is a very special thing. Every sport has a Mecca, and Badminton is ours. I've watched Badminton get bigger each year, but to me it's always the biggest and most awe-inspiring and impressive occasion there is."

The events are extremely demanding on both horse and rider. Along with a jumping test and two days of dressage, riders and mounts compete in speed and endurance tests over 17 miles of road and track, including a two-and-a-half-mile steeplechase and a four-and-a-half-mile cross-country event. Top prize is the coveted Whitbread Trophy, which Captain Mark Phillips has won four times. And if sweating horses and their mud-spattered riders aren't your cup of tea, the 250-plus stalls, which sell most everything from boots and saddles to jewelry and top hats, will certainly have something to suit everyone's taste and pocketbook.

And what about the royal element at Badminton? you ask. Well, eagle-eyed royal observers have been rewarded in past years by visions of the Queen happily standing up to her ankles in mud by a tough jump, or of Prince Philip stalking around the course deep in conversation with Prince Michael of Kent. Along with the senior royals, Badminton also attracts the younger members of the family. The Duchess of Kent's daughter, Lady Helen Windsor, together with Princess Margaret's own Viscount Linley and Lady Sarah Armstrong-Jones, all take the opportunity to watch this top event. Although there is a royal box in the dressage and jumping area, members of the Royal Family all wander around very informally, so be discreetly prepared to run into a royally familiar face.

- *Dates:* Second Thursday, Friday, Saturday, and Sunday of the month.

- *Venue:* Badminton Park, Avon.

- *Getting There:* By Car—Junction 18 on the M4, then follow the blue-and-white RAC signs or yellow AA signs.

- *Getting In:* Entry tickets (per car) cost £22 for all four days, £6 each for the dressage and show-jumping, and £13 for the cross-country. Grandstand seats vary between £3 and £7.

The Royals at Polo

 The heir to the throne stealing a kiss from his pretty wife, Prince William running pell-mell through the pony lines, the Duke of York tickling the red-haired Duchess under the ribs, Prince Philip listening to the radio, the Queen and the Queen Mother watching intently as the Prince of Wales attempts a goal—these are a few of the royal sights the visitor can expect on a trip to the Guards' Polo Club at Smith's Lawn, Windsor Great Park.

Two other elite polo clubs exist at which Prince Charles will compete—Cirencester Park Club and Cowdray Park Club—but the most accessible and by far the most popular venue is undoubtedly the Guards' Club at Windsor. It is here that some of the best informal photographs of the Royal Family—especially of Diana and Charles—have been taken. A trip can pay endless dividends to the royal watcher; not only do you have the pleasure of watching the sport of kings played in the superb setting of Windsor Park, you will also see Prince Charles at full gallop; his polo manager (and the Duchess of York's father), Major Ronald Ferguson, striding around the grounds; and often Princess Diana watching a few chukkers with her friends.

Polo at Windsor

The Prince is a passionate polo player and appears regularly for Les Diables Bleus, the Maple Leafs, and the England second team. It is no coincidence that when he plans his year with the royal courtiers at Kensington Palace, Major Ferguson sits to his right, next to his private secretary. Charles's diary is actually built around his polo engagements, which can be up to five a week. For the Prince the enjoyment of the sport is made clear by his need to keep fit and to get away from the royal grind. "I need exercise to be in the right frame of mind to be of most assistance to everyone else," he explains. "If I can have a game of polo I feel five hundred times better in my mental outlook, but without some form of exercise I get terribly jaded and below par."

Prince Philip, a superb player in his day until an injury prevented further involvement, and Lord Mountbatten, Charles's uncle who was killed by an IRA bomb in 1979, first introduced the young Prince to the game. In turn, he will undoubtedly bring his own sons to the sport when they are old enough, and even at their tender ages they are already being taught how to ride properly. It is a measure of the Prince's dedication that he went off to play polo on the day Prince Harry was born, though what his wife thought about this we are not told.

Major Ferguson, who runs the Guards' Polo Club virtually single-handed, explains the fascination for the game as being bound up with its sheer difficulty. "You've got to maneuver a horse galloping at twenty-eight miles an hour, and at the same time hit a very small bouncing ball through a goal with a long stick, while your opponent is trying to hook your stick and ride you off. . . . It's very dangerous, but the fact it is so frightfully difficult is half the thrill."

Polo is almost as old as horsemanship itself. Legend has it that Hannibal and his officers played a ferocious version using the heads of defeated army chiefs. Today a plain white ash ball is used. Each team has four players; numbers one and two are forwards, number three (usually the team's best player) stays midfield, and number four (the Prince's normal position) hovers at the back. The game is divided into six periods, referred to by their Indian name of chukkers. Actual play time is just 42 minutes, six periods of seven minutes each, though the time-clock is stopped whenever a foul occurs and is restarted when play commences. At the end of seven minutes a bell is rung and the chukker continues until the ball goes out of play, though if a ball is still in play after 30 seconds a second bell is rung and the chukker ends. The aim of the game is to hit the ball between the goalposts at either end of the ground, making it a sort of equestrian hockey match.

At half-time the crowd is invited to walk onto the polo ground to tread in the divots of grass churned up by the players' ponies. Here is your best chance to rub shoulders with the Princess of Wales or the Duchess of York as they come onto the field to help with repairs.

During the game the Princess and the other royal guests can easily be spotted from the spectator stands. They usually sit in the covered royal box or, if the weather is fine, in the open-air members enclosure. Games start at 3:00 P.M., but to make the most of the outing arrive early and bring a picnic lunch with a bottle of champagne to enjoy while reclining on the grass. If at around 2:30 you happen to wander over to the pony lines, you may catch sight of a shirtless Prince of Wales chatting with Major Ferguson about the horses he is due to ride in the game. A visitor will soon know if the Prince has arrived by watching for photographers pointing their cameras in one direction. For years he has come to the games in a blue Aston Martin convertible, while Princess Diana usually arrives shortly after the game has started and makes her way to the royal box.

Frequently the Princess is called upon to present the trophies or medallions at the match's end. There is nothing stuffy or formal about these ceremonies. The crowd comes onto the field to form a semicircle around the players and officials. A table is normally carried out and the honors laid upon it. Each player walks forward for his medallion and a handshake from the Princess. The last person to receive an award is the Prince of Wales, and it has now become a royal tradition that he kisses the Princess to the cheers of the crowd. On the Sunday after Ascot week (see June), the Guards' Club stands are usually filled to capacity to watch the Queen's Cup match, after which the Queen herself presents the awards.

Occasionally Prince Charles will walk about and chat with various members of the crowd; many an American tourist has had his vacation made by a few unexpected words from the charming Prince.

If you would like to see the Prince and Princess leave— always in their separate cars—stand on the roadside by the pony lines.

- *Dates and Times:* Normally Wednesday and Thursday and most weekends during the season, which runs from April to July, starting at 3:00 P.M.

- *Venues: Guards' Polo Club,* Smith's Lawn, Windsor Great Park, Englefield Green, Egham, Surrey (tel. 0784–34212); *Cowdray Park,* Midhurst, West Sussex (tel. 073081–3257); *Cirencester Park,* Cirencester, Gloucestershire (tel. 0285–3225).

- *Getting In:* Each of the above polo grounds has a minimal entry charge of between £2 and £6 per person.

MAY

The month of flowers, May finds the thoughts of the Englishman turning to his garden, and the evening air is filled with the sound of lawn mowers and sprinklers. The Royal Family also enjoys the simple pleasures of the garden, with its social highlight, the Chelsea Flower Show. Polo continues to provide some much-needed exercise for the energetic Prince Charles, and the eventing season is in full swing, offering numerous possible sitings of Princess Anne, Captain Mark Phillips, plus novice eventer Princess Michael—or, at the very least, plenty of fresh country air.

Royal Windsor Show

 Held in the shadow of Windsor Castle, the Royal Windsor Show is the royal equivalent of inviting the neighbors into your backyard. Every year the Queen kindly allows her land to be invaded by a small army of horse boxes, craft booths, and side shows. The hostess herself is often seen with her gold Leica camera, taking photographs of Prince Philip competing in the carriage-driving events at which he excels, or simply watching the show-jumping. Unlike horse shows such as Badminton, the emphasis here is on appearance and breeding rather than endurance and stamina over the jumps. Princess Anne and Captain Mark Phillips attend, as do Prince and Princess Michael of Kent—the carriage driving is their interest—and sometimes the Queen Mother will be seen as well.

The occasion is the show-jumping equivalent of Badminton in terms of the number of royals who attend, largely as a result of its nearness to Windsor Castle. Wandering around the site, a discerning visitor is practically honor-bound to spot some member of the Royal Family, be it Prince Philip reviewing his horses, the Queen in brogues and green rain gear sitting in a deck chair watching the events, or even little Zara Phillips making the rounds of the stalls. Just as a sailor can tell he is nearing land by the sight of seagulls, so you can tell where the royals are by the activity of the press photographers.

- **Dates:** Second Thursday, Friday, Saturday, and Sunday of the month.
- **Venue:** Windsor Castle, Windsor, Royal Berkshire.
- **Getting There:** See "Easter at Windsor" in *April.*

Chelsea Flower Show

In former years as closely bound up with snob appeal as gardening zeal, the Chelsea Flower Show today provides a rather pricey—and horrendously crowded—opportunity to see an amazing number of beautiful flowers and inspired gardening designs all under a gigantic marquee set up on the grounds of the Royal Hospital on the Chelsea Embankment. On the evening before the show opens, the Queen and other members of the Royal Family, including the Prince and Princess of Wales and the Queen's sister, Princess Margaret, all pay a private visit. They can be seen entering and leaving the show in their limousines. Except for a few invited members of the Royal Horticultural Society, there is no admittance for the general public. Likewise, the first day of the show is for R.H.S. members only.

Many royals are keen gardeners, particularly the Queen Mother, who has created a beautiful walled garden on a barren site at her remote Scottish home, the Castle of Mey. Roses, magnolias, and azaleas bloom in staggering abundance in her sheltered retreat, and she admits to enjoying nothing more in the summer than to sit outside with a few handpicked friends and enjoy a quiet picnic.

Prince Charles, too, has been blessed with a green thumb, and has transformed his formerly lackluster garden at Highgrove into a charming plot of wildflower meadows, a well-stocked vegetable area, and hidden shaded spots where the Prince can write letters or simply sit and think. He especially enjoys coming to the Chelsea Flower Show to gain new ideas for his own gardens. On the roof of his London home of Kensington Palace, the Prince has created a garden hideaway

Chelsea Flower Show

where he and Princess Diana can sometimes spend summer afternoons, cooking barbecues and sunbathing.

Once one of the high spots of the London social season, the Chelsea Flower Show was a place where young artistocrats could be seen on the lookout for a suitable spouse as well as the latest strain of climbing rose. Now it is gardeners and those who love the outdoors who proliferate—with a vengeance— though the feeling of blue-blooded anticipation still lingers. There are still grand old ladies who arrive in chauffeur-driven Rolls and trail around the stands with the head gardener in tow, ordering vast quantities of whatever takes their eye. Over the years there have been moments of unbridled extravagance, as when Queen Victoria's son, the Prince of Wales—who never ever did a thing by halves—purchased an entire garden for an undisclosed amount. The most impressive spending in recent years was for a stand of rare orchids, a purchase totalling in the region of $20,000.

- **_Date and Time:_** The show opens on the third Tuesday of May. The Queen's visit is on the previous evening; check _The Times,_ the _Star,_ the *Independent,* and the *Telegraph* for the exact time. The first day of the show is for R.H.S. members only.

- *Venue:* Royal Hospital Grounds, Chelsea Embankment, London.

- *Getting There: By Tube*—Sloane Square.

- *Getting In:* £24 will buy membership in the Royal Horticultural Society plus two tickets for the members' private view, with an additional £5 enrollment fee; or simply pay £14, £12, or £9 respectively to gain admission on the last three days of the show.

Horse Trials

The eventing season is now well under way. Below are listed a few of the many shows which occur this month, all of which have in the past been graced by the royal presence.

Longleat Novice Trials

Dressage, show jumping, and cross-country across undulating parkland.

- *Date:* May 20.

- *Venue:* Longleat House, Warminster, Wiltshire (tel. 09853–551).

- *Getting There: By Car*—just off the A362 Warminster-Frome road; all entrances are marked.

Windsor Horse Trials

Riders jumping against the clock; the British Open Junior Championship.

- *Dates:* Third Friday to Sunday of the month.

- *Venue:* Windsor Great Park, Windsor, Royal Berkshire.

- *Getting There:* See "Easter at Windsor" in *April.*

Chepstow Horse Trials

Small meet for mainly Welsh competitors; jumps over solid timber fences.

- *Dates:* Last weekend of the month.

- *Venue:* Chepstow Racecourse and Piercefield Park, Gwent, Wales.

- *Getting There: By Car*—one mile north of Chepstow on the A466 Monmouth road, two miles from Exit 22 on the M4.

JUNE

A time of freely flowing champagne, strawberries and cream, pedigreed horses, and thoroughbred tennis players, June is the height of the English social season and a month when the Royal Family is out in force. An additional bonus is that none of the major events is far from London. Royal Ascot, the Derby, and Wimbledon all provide a feast of color, excitement, and frivolity, while the Queen's Birthday Parade is royal pageantry at its very best. June is without doubt the one month when in the space of an afternoon you can stand next to the Queen at Ascot, then watch Princess Diana give her husband an affectionate kiss after a hard-fought polo match.

The Derby

A day of great excitement and of the most famous flat race in the calendar, the Derby (pronounced "Darby") finds the English landed gentry mingling with the working classes as gypsies tell fortunes and betters lose them. For a week before the big race, Epsom Downs racecourse is invaded by scores of gypsies from all over Britain. Offering a kaleidoscope of sights and sounds, the day is one of contrasts, from the super-rich arriving on the course in helicopters to tinkers turning up in their traditional pony and traps; from jobless women selling lucky heather outside the racecourse to millionaires sipping Krug champagne inside.

The highlight of the day, besides the race itself, is the arrival of the Royal Family. The Queen, the Queen Mother, Prince Philip, Prince Charles, Princess Diana, and Princess Alexandra are all regulars. They normally arrive at 1:00 P.M. and drive down the course in limousines. The royals have their own box, and those fortunate spectators positioned opposite can observe their movements through binoculars. Unlike at Ascot, however (which occurs later this month), the Royal Family does not mingle with the Derby crowd.

At about 3:10 the royals slowly walk from their enclosure along the course to the paddock, where they view the horses due to run in the big race at 3:30. The Queen Mother, who suffers from leg ulcers, is usually taken back to the royal box by car, and most often gets the biggest cheer from the crowd lining the route. Ironically, when the race starts, the Queen sits inside the royal box, preferring to watch the outcome on television.

On departure, the royals once more drive slowly down the course in a procession of vast, gleaming limousines—in itself quite a sight.

- *Date and Time:* First Wednesday in the month, with the race starting at 3:30 P.M.

- *Venue:* Espom Downs, Surrey.

- *Getting There: By Train*—frequent trains run from London's Waterloo Station to Epsom, after which it is a ten-minute walk to the course. Three railway stations in Epsom are equidistant from the racecourse—Epsom Town, Tattenham Corner, and Epsom Downs—though there is a bus service to the course from the last. *By Car*—though the course is only 17 miles from London, driving is not recommended because of the huge crowds and difficulties in parking.

- *Getting In:* Hundreds of thousands of spectators make the annual pilgrimage to Epsom, so if you wish to get a good view arrive early, certainly before midday. Grandstand tickets can be purchased on the day, and cost about £12, with an extra £4 fee if you wish to follow the Queen and her family to the paddock. Tickets for the enclosures cost between £4 and £6, though you can also pay £30 in advance for the best grandstand seats in Anglesey Enclosure; book through Keith Prowse, whose New York branch is at 234 West 44th St., Suite 902, New York, NY 10036 (212–398–1430; 800–223–4446).

The Queen's Birthday Parade

Commonly known as Trooping of the Color, the Queen's Birthday Parade is one of the most spectacular displays of pageantry anywhere in the world. It is actually a combination of two ancient military maneuvers, Trooping the Color and Mounting the Queen's Guard. Each move is an intricate display of marching and counter-marching so complicated it cannot be written down and must be passed on by word of mouth from generation to generation. Despite this difficulty, year after year the maneuvers are performed with perfect military precision.

The Queen was actually born on April 21, but the second Saturday in June is deemed her "official" birthday—possibly because it stands a better chance of having good weather—and is the day when she leads this major review of her ceremonial troops on Horse Guards Parade, in central London. For more

Trooping the Color

than 30 years the Queen rode sidesaddle at the head of her regiments, accompanied by the royal dukes, including Prince Philip and the Prince of Wales, both honorary colonels-in-chief of Guards regiments. In 1987, however, she decided for the first time to ride in a carriage after her customary mount, Burmese— a gift from the Royal Canadian Mounted Police—went into retirement.

The Queen's role in the ceremony is not only as monarch but as colonel-in-chief of the seven regiments of the Household Division. Like nearly every aspect of British military ceremony, the parade stems from a practical purpose. The term "trooping" means "saluting by beat of drum," hence the significance of that instrument throughout the ceremony. When Britain's first standing army was formed several centuries ago, it was important that the soldiers—many of whom were foreign mercenaries—knew whom they were fighting for. The standard, or color, was paraded through the regiment every night before a battle with the drums playing in order to instill a sense of camaraderie and fighting spirit.

Altogether more than 200 horses and 2,000 men take part in the two-hour display, including detachments of the mounted regiments of the Household Cavalry and the Massed Mounted Bands. The Queen is the only woman on parade during the ceremony; nothing escapes her practiced eye—after all, she has performed every year since 1952—and many is the time an admonishing memo from her private secretary has been dispatched to the officer of a particular regiment complaining about some aspect or other. The sovereign's own impeccable standards of discipline were superbly displayed in 1982 when she brought her mount under control after a youth fired five blank cartridges at her from close range.

The ceremony begins when the Queen leaves Buckingham Palace and rides down the tree-lined Mall to Horse Guards Parade, arriving exactly as the clock strikes 11:00—although on occasion the clock has been timed to strike as the Queen arrives and not the other way around! The National Anthem is played and a 41-gun salute fired. Then, riding the length of the front rank, she inspects the parade, itself a complex series of well-defined drill movements with eight contingents of foot guards, each with three officers and 70 other ranks. The Massed Bands of the Guards Division, together with the Corps of Pipes and Drums, parade in front of the garden wall which borders onto the rear of Number 10 Downing Street, the residence of the Prime Minister.

The Queen Mother and other members of the Royal Family always watch the ceremony from the Horse Guards building. They stand in the major general's office, exactly above the center arch of the building. Amid all the pageantry there is a very human touch as the Queen passes beneath the window where the Queen Mother is watching; she always gives her mother a smart salute which is returned with a smile and a wave.

The massed bands, in the meantime, give a splendid display of marching in slow and quick time, beginning with the traditional slow march, "Les Huguenots." Once the color has been trooped through all the ranks, the parade marches past the saluting Queen. As the color is carried past, it is lowered in deference to the monarch. Then the entire parade is led by the Queen back along the Mall to Buckingham Palace.

But the spectacle does not end there. Shortly after 1:00, the Queen leads the rest of the Royal Family onto the palace balcony to watch a flypast by the Royal Air Force, which gives the determined royal watchers an excellent opportunity to see the whole family together on the much-photographed balcony.

- **Date and Time:** Traditionally the second Saturday of the month, starting at 11:00 A.M.

- **Venue:** Horse Guards Parade, London.

- **Getting There:** By Tube—St. James's Park, Green Park, and Charing Cross.

- **How to See:** Only 7,000 people are admitted to the 11 stands that ring Horse Guards Parade. Around 3,000 seats are taken up by various dignitaries and military VIPs, leaving only 4,000 for the public. You can apply for no more than two tickets, and must do so between January 1 and March 1; apply to the Brigade Major, Household Division, Horse Guards, Whitehall, London, SW1A 2AX, enclosing a stamped, self-addressed envelope. Tickets are free.

  For those who are denied admission there are two consolation prizes: There are dress rehearsals, on the preceding two Saturdays, with the Duke of Edinburgh taking the salute on the second. If you specify that you wish to be considered for the rehearsals, your name will go into further ballots.

  If you don't win a ticket you have the choice of either watching the ceremony on television—which provides excellent coverage—or of standing with the crowds who line the Mall to watch the procession go by and to see the Royal Family on the balcony at Buckingham Palace. A pair of binoculars is recommended.

The Garter Ceremony

 The Order of the Garter is the most prestigious of all the orders of knighthood, and every Monday of Ascot week the Queen and other members of the Royal Family attend the Garter Service at Windsor. A procession of cloaked and plumed figures walks slowly down from Windsor Castle to St. George's Chapel for a service of Thanksgiving for the Order of the Garter, an order of chivalry founded in the 14th century by Edward III, who wanted an elite body of knights to swear personal allegiance to him.

A charming myth recounts that Joan, the Fair Maid of Kent and wife of the Earl of Salisbury, accidently let her garter slip from her leg during a celebration ball. As this deed was usually associated with ladies of loose morals, everyone laughed at her discomfiture. The gallant King, however, retrieved the garter and tied it around his own leg, uttering the words: "*Honi soit qui mal y pense*"—"Evil to him who evil thinks." The words have become the motto of the order, whose emblem is a dark blue velvet garter edged with gold.

Inspired to create the order by the example of the legendary Knights of the Round Table, Edward III limited the number of Knights Companions to just 24 (in addition to the royal knights, who bring the tally up to 33). Today Prince Philip is a member, as is Prince Charles. There are also a number of extra knights in honor of foreign royalty, including the emperor of Japan, the kings of Belgium, Sweden, and Norway, and ex-Queen Juliana of the Netherlands (known as a Lady of the Garter), one of the few women to be so honored.

The choice of knights is non-political, and is entirely left for the reigning monarch to decide. If there is a vacancy in this elite order, a new knight is installed and invested in the Throne Room at Windsor Castle on the day of the ceremony, when the Queen will buckle a garter to the knight's left leg. The new knight then joins the Queen and other members of the order for a procession through the castle courtyard to St. George's Chapel, where the full ceremony of installation takes place. Over the centuries there have been more than 900 members of the order, each with his own individual coat of arms.

- **Date and Time:** Normally on the Monday before Royal Ascot.

- **Venue:** St. George's Chapel, Windsor Castle, Windsor, Royal Berkshire.

- **Getting There:** See "Easter at Windsor" in *April.*

- **How to See:** There is no public admission to the ceremony in St. George's Chapel, but limited numbers are admitted to the castle grounds to watch the procession. Demand is heavy and spectators are selected by ballot. Apply early in the year to the Lord Chamberlain's Office, St. James's Palace, London SW1A 1BE.

Royal Ascot

 The four-day horse meeting that is Royal Ascot is the pinacle of the English social calendar. It is a superb opportunity for star spotting and royal watching. The days pass in an orgy of champagne, smoked salmon, chauffeured Rolls-Royces, pretty women done up to the nines, and gentlemen perspiring in top hat and tails. Amid it all are members of the Royal Family, strolling among the racegoers as they study some of the world's best horseflesh.

A tradition inaugurated by Queen Anne in 1711, Royal Ascot was allowed to fall by the wayside on her death just three years later, before being revived in style by the Duke of Cumberland, son of George II. By the time George III (the very king the American colonists later rebelled against so successfully) had ascended to the throne in 1760, Ascot was once more a social and sporting occasion of the highest order, where the ladies came to parade their extravagant fashions, the men to win or lose their fortunes.

The Royal Family attended regularly until 1861, when Queen Victoria went into near-permanent mourning over the death of her beloved Prince Albert and never again set foot upon the turf. However, her exuberant son, the Prince of Wales (later Edward VII) was a highly successful racegoer who rarely missed a meeting. His example has been enthusiastically kept up by the Royal Family. The present Queen attended her first Ascot in 1945, as a young girl of 18. Since then she has attended each year except 1955, when a national rail strike marred the festivities. Prince Philip is not nearly so keen. He normally stays for the first race, then sidles away to watch the polo at Windsor while listening to a cricket commentary on the latest England Test match on his car radio.

For the royal watcher, the first sight of the Royal Family is during the traditional carriage parade down the course. The Queen and her guests leave Windsor Castle, where the monarch is in residence, in a car procession at 1:35 P.M., then drive along the famous Long Drive to Ascot Gate of Windsor Great Park. Here they change over to the carriages, leaving at 1:45 precisely for the slow drive along the course.

It's not just the royals who parade along the course, however, as a number of house guests will join them in their splendid carriages, a practice which sometimes gives the media a chance to guess who is romancing whom. In 1985 there was great excitement when the pretty, red-haired Miss Sarah Ferguson accompanied Prince Andrew in a carriage. She made headlines as "Prince Andrew's New Girlfriend," and for once the journalists were right. Less than a year later the couple were engaged, and admitted that romance had blossomed during Royal Ascot week.

Though the Queen's carriage drive is easily seen from most parts of the course, the best vantage point is the public enclosure opposite the winning post. This is not the only glimpse of the Royal Family afforded to the public, however. After each race the Queen and other members of the clan will walk down to the paddock, mingling with the racegoers as they carefully eye up the parade of thoroughbred horses. Two white lines about six feet apart mark the path the Queen follows, and hordes of spectators line either side to watch the royals walk past. The regular Ascotonians will concentrate on the younger members of the family—Fergie and Diana, for example—who often wander unrestricted among the smartly dressed crowd.

At around 3:30 the royal watcher has a choice: to stay to the end of the race meeting and observe the Queen, or to go on to the polo match at nearby Smith's Lawn. If they choose the former they will witness, and can join in if they wish, the communal singing, often raucous and high-spirited, around the bandstand at 6:30, where tipsy ladies dance impromptu jigs with top-hatted gentlemen.

If you choose to leave and travel the four miles to the polo match at Smith's Lawn, you will need either to have your own car or to go by taxi. At Smith's Lawn the royal spotter will see Prince Charles displaying his polo prowess once again, most often watched by Princess Diana, Prince Philip, and the Duke and Duchess of York.

- **Dates and Times:** Traditionally the third week in June, from Tuesday to Friday.

- **Venue:** Ascot Racecourse, Ascot, Royal Berkshire.

- **Getting There:** *By Car*—it is best to arrive before noon to avoid the traffic jams. From London get onto the M4, then turn off onto the M25, following signs for Gatwick Airport. Exit at junction 12 and pick up the M3, turning off at junction 3 and taking the A322 for Bracknell. From here follow the signs for Ascot. *By Train*—British Rail operates frequent services to Ascot Station from London's Waterloo Station, and from Guildford and Reading; from there it is an eight-minute walk to the racecourse.

- **Getting In:** Tickets for the course can be bought without formality at the turnstiles, costing between £1 and £12. English visitors who wish to sit in the Royal Enclosure must apply by no later than the end of April to Her Majesty's Representative at the Ascot Office, St. James's Palace, London SW1, giving full names of the applicants (individual applications will be needed for people not belonging to the same family). Americans wanting a seat in the Royal Enclosure should apply to the American Embassy, 24 Grosvenor Square, London W1, by the end of March.

  In addition to Ascot itself, each year a limited number of tickets are issued to allow the public to watch the royal party exchange their cars for carriages, which takes place at the Ascot Gate of Windsor Great Park. For tickets, write early in the year to: The Deputy Ranger, Crown Estate Office, Windsor Great Park, Berkshire, SL4 2HT.

  Applications for boxes should be made to: Grand Stand Office, Ascot Racecourse, Ascot, Berkshire.

Wimbledon

 The Royal Family has long been associated with the game of tennis, and in particular with the All-England Lawn Tennis and Croquet Club. England's First Family has been attending the championships ever since the Prince of Wales, later George V, accepted the first presidency of the club in 1907. His son, George VI (then Duke of York), created a stir by playing in a doubles match in the 1926 championships. Since then, the club has always been honored with a royal president, currently the Duke of Kent, who, with his wife, regularly presents the prizes at the conclusion of the tournament.

Though none of the Royal Family actually compete in the tournament these days, current royal interest is not simply idle curiosity. Many family members—especially the women—play themselves. The Princess of Wales, the Duchess of York, the Duchess of Gloucester, and—of course—Princess Michael of Kent all play regularly at the exclusive Queen's Club in London. Princess Michael is so keen, she can often be spotted setting off from Kensington Palace at dawn for the courts. But the female royals can't take all the credit; the Duchess of Kent's son, Lord Nicholas Windsor, is a fine player who has done remarkably well in amateur competitions.

The royal ladies, especially, are regularly seen taking their seats in the Royal Box on the Center Court to watch an encounter between the giants of the tennis world. Before her wedding the Duchess of York—then Miss Sarah Ferguson—took her friends along to watch the proceedings in an attempt to forget the cares of organizing her big day. Princess Diana, too, is a familiar sight during the two weeks of the tournament.

The club was initially founded in 1868 as a croquet club, with tennis merely constituting a sideline. These days there are no less than 18 grass courts, including the Center Court and Number One Court, as well as 11 hard courts. In the Center Court, the showpiece of world tennis, there is space for 14,000 spectators (including standing room for 2,100), while the Number One Court has 6,286 seats and standing room for 1,000. Throughout the championships about 350,000 spectators pass through the turnstiles, and tons of strawberries, gallons of cream, and an ocean of champagne (not to mention beer) are consumed by the throng.

- **Dates and Times:** The opening games start six weeks before the first Monday in August, around June 22, and the tournament usually finishes on or about July 5; first matches of the day start at 12:30. Play generally stops around 8:30.

- **Venue:** All-England Lawn Tennis and Croquet Club, Church Road, London SW19 (tel. 01–946 2244).

- **Getting There:** By Tube—District Line to Wimbledon Park or Southfields; from the former the grounds are just an eight-minute walk, well signposted (or just follow the crowds); from Southfields there is bus transport.

- **Getting In:** A combined ballot for tickets for Center Court and Number One Court is held each year; applicants should send a stamped, self-addressed envelope for an application form by the end of

December to: The All-England Lawn Tennis and Croquet Club, Church Road, Wimbledon, London SW19 5AE. Some tickets may be available to overseas clubs. In addition, 300 tickets for reserved seats on Center Court and 500 on Number One Court are sold at the grounds each day. Admission to the other courts and the grounds is through the turnstiles at Church Road or Somerset Road. After 5:00 P.M., admission is reduced.

JULY

English weather may be unpredictable during this mid-summer month, but the royal regimen never varies. The Royal Family forsakes the capital during July and heads for the provinces. The Queen travels north to Scotland on a State visit for the first week of the month, while the Queen Mother spends two weeks in Norfolk. Prince Charles is well occupied, as the polo season is still in full swing, with a number of international matches scheduled.

The Ceremony of the Keys

 During the first week in July the Queen is resident in one of her favorite cities, Edinburgh, the capital of Scotland. She stays in the Palace of Holyroodhouse, located at the end of the Royal Mile (which leads up to Edinburgh Castle). Throughout the week the soverign carries out a number of official duties, almost all in a delightfully informal atmosphere.

On her arrival the one annual set piece—the Ceremony of the Keys—is performed. Here the Queen is handed the keys of the city by the Lord Lieutenant, before she inspects an immaculate guard of honor wearing the distinctive Black Watch tartan. Unlike its magnificent (but non-royal) counterpart at the Tower of London, the Ceremony of the Keys consists simply of the Lord Lieutenant handing the keys to the Queen on a red velvet cushion. These she duly accepts before handing them back. The ritual, which takes place in the palace forecourt, can be seen from the wrought-iron palace railings; no tickets are needed.

- *Date and Time:* First week in July, just after the Queen has arrived at Holyroodhouse, usually in the afternoon.

- *Venue:* Palace of Holyroodhouse, Cannongate, Edinburgh, Scotland (tel. 031–556 7371).

Holyrood House

The Thistle Ceremony

 During the Queen's week in Edinburgh there is often a separate ceremony if a new Knight of the Thistle is to be installed. This historic ceremony takes place in the Thistle Chapel in St. Giles Cathedral during the first two days of the Queen's stay. Both the ceremony and its setting call to mind Scotland's proud history. The ceremony of the Scottish Order of Knighthood, a supremely elite order whose members total just 16, has changed only slightly since the order was founded by James II in 1687. The Queen Mother made history by being the first woman ever to be admitted to the Order of the Thistle, at the express wish of her husband, King George VI.

The service is private, but the procession can be watched from the High Street and from Parliament Square in front of the cathedral. Promptly at 11:15 the Queen, Prince Philip, and Prince Charles arrive at the cathedral to be received by the Minister and the Chancellor of the Thistle, currently Lord Home (a former Prime Minister). The royal party, resplendent in dark green velvet robes and plumed hats, then enter the cathedral to a fanfare sounded by Her Majesty's Household Trumpeters. While the public is not admitted to the service, visitors can nonetheless hear the psalms and the Queen's words during the solemn ceremony, which is broadcast outside on a loudspeaker.

The setting for this venerable ceremony, the lovely Thistle Chapel, is a gem of architecture, but is not nearly as ancient as it looks. The installations of new knights to the order used to be held in Holyroodhouse until the early years of this century. Then, Edward VII suggested building a Thistle Chapel attached to the cathedral, resulting in the beautiful chapel with its colorful roof, exquisite stonework, and splendidly carved stalls.

Stowe Horse Trials

 Princess Anne, Captain Mark Phillips, and Princess Michael of Kent regularly attend these prestigious horse trials on the grounds of one of England's top schools. The trials themselves consist of dressage, show-jumping, and cross-country across flat farmland and woodland.

- **Date:** Second weekend in July.

- **Venue:** Stowe School, Buckinghamshire.

- **Getting There:** *By Car*—Stowe School is one and a half miles north of Buckingham, and is signposted from the A43 at Silverstone, and from Buckingham itself.

Sandringham Flower Show

 A pleasant mixture of garden show, bazaar, craft exhibit, and amusement fair, the Sandringham Flower Show is always graced by the kindly presence of the Queen Mother. She will often take along one of her grandchildren, such as Prince Charles or Lady Sarah Armstrong-Jones, to enjoy the quintessentially English atmosphere. The show sees gardeners from the area competing for cups and trophies awarded for the best produce and flowers, and you'll find an abundance of tents with tables laid out with arrays of homemade cakes, jams, honey, and local crafts. On a pleasant summer day there can be few things more relaxing than pottering about the grounds—with one eye on the royals, of course—looking over the handsewn quilts or stocking up on a few Christmas presents for friends back home.

Normally the Queen Mother arrives at around 11:00 and goes from tent to tent looking over the array of produce. One year Prince Charles walked behind her with a basket in hand, buying flowers, jars of honey, and teddy bears for his two sons. As the royals walk through the show grounds, crowds line the path, and the Queen Mother seems to have a word for everyone—though Prince Charles is not far behind when it comes to chatting with well-wishers. This meet-the-people walk is one of the longest the royals ever undertake on a regular basis, and can often last up to 90 minutes, depending on the weather and the Queen Mother's health.

As a matter of course, visitors come from miles around to get a glimpse of Britain's favorite great-grandmother, so it's wise to be in position early. And if you carry a bunch of flowers or wear bright clothing, you are more likely to be approached for a quick word.

- **Date:** Last Wednesday in July.

- **Venue:** Sandringham House, King's Lynn, Norfolk (tel. 0553–772675).

- **Getting There:** See "Sandringham" in *January.*

The Kings Lynn Festival

 The Queen Mother is the patron of the Kings Lynn Festival, founded in 1951. For two weeks in July she stays at nearby Sandringham House, which she uses as a base to visit various exhibitions staged during Festival Week at the end of the month. She makes a point of visiting the Fermow center, and obviously enjoys viewing the many art shows and displays which take place. There is no set timetable for her visits, however, and many onlookers have been surprised when doing the rounds of an exhibition to find a familiar figure in pale blue just ahead, handbag on arm.

As the program changes from year to year, a pattern to her perambulations cannot be guaranteed, but anyone taking in the cultural delights of this festival stands a very good chance of bumping into the Queen Mum.

- **Date:** July 24 to August 1.

- **Venue:** Kings Lynn, Norfolk.

- **Getting There:** See above.

AUGUST _____

The polo ponies return to their stables for a well-deserved rest, and everyone's thoughts turn to vacation time and picnics. Members of the Royal Family go on vacation, too, with the royal yacht *Britannia* acting as a floating home away from home. The first port of call is the Isle of Wight for the Cowes Regatta. Then, the majestic yacht steams away on its journey to the western isles of Scotland.

Cowes Regatta

Cowes Week is the crowning glory of the sailing calendar. For more than 150 years, Cowes, once a tiny backwater on the Isle of Wight, has been the annual August playground for European royalty. It makes a colorful sight, with thousands of spectators thronging the shores, all eyes on the scores of yachts of every

Cowes Regatta

size and shape scudding across the Solent, sails billowing and blossoming in the breeze. For the past 30 years the royal yacht *Britannia* has dominated the scene, her myriad dress flags fluttering gaily, and her invariably new coat of paint gleaming like a beacon. The spectators and competitors who converge here every year have fun watching the nautical spectacle, which may include Prince Philip at the helm of his tiny racing fifteen *Cowslip,* Princess Anne and Prince Edward crewing on one of the bigger yachts, Prince Charles in his black wet-suit splashing along on a windsurfer, or Prince Andrew going for a spin in a speedboat.

The royal tradition at Cowes dates back to the early nineteenth century, when the hedonistic George IV, then Prince Regent, first heard about the delights of a newly founded yacht club in Cowes. In 1817 he forsook his favorite seaside resort of Brighton to see what all the fuss was about. The fuss was subsequently deemed worthy, and as a result the word "royal" was added to the club name, becoming the Royal Yacht Squadron, and all society flocked to watch. In 1826 came the first race for a cup, a rather ignominious beginning as it turned out, since a free-for-all developed when two boats collided. A year later the inauguration of a King's Cup produced celebrations described by the local papers as "continuing until the blacksmith of night struck the anvil of morn." British and foreign monarchs alike made their annual pilgrimage to Cowes. Queen Victoria and Prince Albert particularly loved the event, not surprisingly, given the proximity of Osborne House to Cowes.

But while the Queen loved to watch the sailing, it was her excitement-loving son the Prince of Wales, later Edward VII, who really set the stamp of glamour on Cowes. It came as a welcome end to his hectic London season, and he also found it useful as an away-from-Court vacation with his current love, the music-hall temptress Lily Langtry. For several years running she visited a small cottage opposite West Cowes Castle.

The Prince gave a considerable impetus to yacht racing not only by his generous patronage, but also—and much more importantly—by his enthusiastic participation. For many years he owned a number of racing yachts, the last and best known being the cutter *Britannia,* which, in a career stretching from 1893 to 1935, collected an awesome 231 first prizes. Edward reputedly loved this elegant craft, and described her as being "as handy and lively as a kitten." On his death the *Britannia* passed to his son George V, who was equally enamored with her. Sir Philip Hunlike, the King's racing master, said of the relationship between yacht and royal master, "Aboard the *Britannia,* the King was like a schoolboy home for a holiday. He loved the old yacht; he enjoyed winning but was a splendid loser."

For the past three decades Prince Philip has nobly carried on the royal Cowes tradition—he is Admiral of the Squadron—but he is the first to admit that a Dragon Class boat given as a wedding present, and the tiny *Cowslip,* kept on board the present-day *Britannia,* are not in the same league as Edward VII's *Britannia.* As he says himself, "No one could bring themselves to look upon an overgrown dinghy and a class boat with a three-man crew as royal yachts, certainly not as direct successors to the majestic old *Britannia.*"

For him and other members of the Royal Family, Cowes Week is just the first stage in an annual vacation on *Britannia* that takes in a cruise around the Western Isles of Scotland and finishes in the peace and privacy of Balmoral. *Britannia* plays an essential part in the royal summer break. She is always given a fresh coat of paint in the home port of Portsmouth to prepare her for Cowes Week, and, when the yacht ties up to a buoy in the Solent, crewmen apply the finishing touches. She rarely misses the Regatta, though in 1987 a major refit forced Prince Philip to stay elsewhere. Normally Princess Alexandra, Angus Ogilvy, and their children are welcome regulars on board, as is Princess Margaret's daughter, Lady Sarah Armstrong-Jones. It is a time, too, to bring girlfriends along, for as one among many guests aboard *Britannia,* they can merge in with the others and not be quite so easily pinpointed by the journalists and photographers. The Princess of Wales visited Cowes in 1980 before her engagement and reportedly had a marvelous time, exploring the yacht and watching her husband-to-be windsurf.

Balls, banquets, banter, and bonhomie are the stuff of Cowes Week, with one night bringing a flamboyant costume party, the next a lighthearted dinner with yachting chums aboard *Britannia.* But sailing is the main attraction, as a teenage Princess Anne explained in her school magazine: "Sailing on a sunny day, with a fresh breeze blowing . . . is the nearest thing to heaven anyone will ever get on this earth. The silence is blissful after you switch off the engine. The only sound is the rush of the water, relaxing and hypnotic, the gentle creak of the rigging, and occasional flap of a lazy sail. . . ."

The racing in the narrow channel between the Isle of Wight and the mainland obviously must be watched through binoculars. Normally the greatest crush of spectators is along one of the banks nearest the Royal Yacht Squadron, where as many as 60 races a day—going off at five-minute intervals—begin. The yachts are divided by a complex set of handicapping rules into 26 classes. The most prestigious and expensive yachts are those contesting the bi-annual Admiral's Cup. This is an international competition that includes races in the Solent, across the English Channel and back, and the Fasnet Race, a 650-mile haul to the southern tip of Ireland and back to Plymouth in Devon.

Cowes Week could be considered the watery equivalent of Ascot. While many visitors are serious yachting enthusiasts, as many again come only for the considerable social scene and the chance to see the Royal Family. Besides the enjoyable occupation of watching the royals luff up, bear away, and hoist the mizzen, as well as perform a number of other nautical maneuvers, the formal highlight of the week is the Royal Yacht Squadron Ball, attended by Prince Philip and other members of the family. This is a private, by-invitation-only affair, though the royal party can be seen walking into the Squadron from outside the clubhouse.

- *Dates:* Usually the first week in August.

- *Venue:* Cowes, Isle of Wight.

- *Getting There:* Ferry or hydrofoil from Southampton to Cowes.

- *Getting In:* More than 12,000 yachting enthusiasts are drawn to Cowes each year for the Regatta, and the small town becomes full to bursting point. Therefore, if you want to make hotel reservations it's wise to do it well in advance, certainly by January or February. For more information about the Cowes Regatta write to the Cowes Combined Clubs Committee, 17–19 Bath Road, Cowes, Isle of Wight P031 7QN (tel. 0983–293303).

The Queen Mother's Birthday Celebration

Like so many occasions associated with the Queen Mother, her birthday celebrations epitomize all that is gracious and charming about the Royal Family. They are informal, relaxed, unstuffy, and entirely predictable. From the red geraniums on the balcony to the Scottish piper who wakes her at 8:00, the routine is changeless.

The Queen Mother's day starts with the piper serenading her under her second-floor bedroom window. As the crowds gather, dozens of well-wishers drop by with cards or bunches of flowers. Then at 11 o'clock the white gates open wide, and the Queen Mother, the Queen, Princess Margaret and her children, Lady Sarah Armstrong-Jones and Viscount Linley, together with the Prince and Princess of Wales and the Duke and Duchess of York, all walk out to greet the crowd. There are smiles all around as the crowd spontaneously bursts into a chorus of "Happy Birthday, Queen Mother," and the Queen, careful not to upstage her parent, beams from the background as the Queen Mother herself nods her thanks and approval. As a matter of fact, it's often hard to know who's having a better time—the crowd, the Queen Mother, or the Royal Family in attendance. The police then usher the children forward to give Britain's favorite great-grandmother homemade birthday cards and yet more flowers. After about five minutes the royal party begins to drift back through the gates, with many a backwards wave. But watch for the odd errant corgi, who will often try to steal the show by wandering around the crowd. Often a royal valet has to usher the dog back inside, a fitting finale to an occasion that leaves everyone smiling.

- *Date:* August 4.
- *Venue:* Clarence House, London.
- *Getting There: By Tube*—Green Park.

Western Islands Cruise

 Britannia usually leaves Cowes on a Monday, with little ceremony, and is under way before 8:00 A.M., followed as always by its attendant destroyer. Then it's off for the islets and inlets of the Scottish west coast, taking the Queen and other members of the Royal Family on board at Southampton. (Unfortunately, the dockyard here is not open to the public.)

In a holiday tradition dating back to Queen Victoria's time, the royal yacht will go out of its way to seek secluded stretches along the west coast of Scotland. For the present Royal Family, however, slacks, sneakers, sandals, and T-shirts are the usual items worn during the cruise, though what the staunchly Victorian Queen would have made of such casual and un-royal apparel does not seem too hard to guess. The present Queen loves this family time so much, she has issued several Christmas cards which feature the family at leisure on *Britannia.*

As far as accommodations go, the Queen and Prince Philip occupy the royal suite at the stern of the yacht. Prince Andrew, Prince Edward, the Duchess of York, and Princess Anne and her two children, Zara and Peter, have guest cabins on the main deck. Prince Charles and Princess Diana usually fly up to join the family at Balmoral later. Breakfast is casual, usually a serve-yourself affair, and lunch is informal as well. But afternoon tea at 4:30 is quite a ceremony; the Queen is reputedly extremely fussy about getting her Darjeeling blend just right. "In our family, everything stops for tea," Prince Charles once remarked. "I have never known a family so addicted to it." Dinner is the main meal of the day, when everyone joins the Queen and Prince Philip at the dinner table.

Barbecues and impromptu picnics are favorite pastimes, and the royals relish these informal feasts on the many isolated beaches of the Scottish Isles. Prince Charles freely admits he got his own taste for barbecues on these trips, where his father is the undisputed master of ceremonies. One year, he recalls, they stopped by the Isle of Uist for a feast upon a "bleak and totally solitary islet, sadly disrupted by millions of midges." Mull and Aran are two other favored picnicking sites, though there is no set pattern. Holiday makers in the Western Isles are often surprised to see the royal party come ashore on their stretch of beach.

Even for an "impromptu" picnic, however, all sorts of preparations have to be made. First, detectives go ahead to check out the proposed beach; no matter how secluded it may seem, it's always best to be sure. Then the royal barge loaded with grills, sausages, chicken, and the rest of the picnic-makings—as well as the royals themselves—arrives at the barbecue site, and for several hours they are on their own, a detective watching from either end of the bay. As one former royal servant says, "They don't mind cooking for and serving themselves, but cleaning up is out."

In between the barbecues and the scuba diving, the deck-hockey and the water-skiing—the Duchess of York once injured her knee in a bad fall—there is the occasional formal visit to be fitted in. However, one visit is made every year that the entire family looks forward to—lunch with the Queen Mother at the Castle of Mey.

Arrival at Scrabster

 This is possibly one of the least known yet most rewarding occasions of the royal year, when the visitor can witness for the only time in the year the Royal Family acting in the capacity of both family and royal court. The day starts early with the royal yacht *Britannia* anchoring off Scrabster Harbor, the Queen's standard flying and scores of dress flags fluttering in the breeze. The narrow road to the quayside is soon packed with locals and visitors who journey down to the waterfront. At 10:50 the Queen Mother pulls up in her black Daimler, while her lady-in-waiting, Ruth, Lady Fermoy—Princess Diana's grandmother—stands nearby. To while away the time, the Queen Mother will chat to local dignitaries resplendent in their kilts, and she usually appears to know the names of half the locals in the crowd.

As the onlookers wait in anticipation, the royal party embarks onto the dark-blue royal barge from the yacht, and are transported to the granite harbor steps. At 11 o'clock sharp—the ritual never varies—the royal party makes its way up the steps, press photographers waiting for a possible slip.

The waiting crowd now witnesses the official form of royal greeting not seen in public on any other occasion. The Queen greets her mother first, then it's Prince Philip's turn. He first kisses his mother-in-law's right cheek, then her left, and finally her hand, before swiftly executing an elegant and courtly bow from the hips. This formal greeting is repeated by all the royal males, although in 1983 the Queen Mother did stand back in surprise from Prince Andrew, now the Duke of York, to exclaim "Oh! I do like your beard!" The royal ladies also follow the kissing routine, but then drop a deep curtsy to the elderly royal. It is fascinating to witness such polite formality at such a relaxed occasion, and it inspired one headline writer to quip, "The Royal Kissogran."

After the harborside greeting, the royal party travels to the nearby Castle of Mey for lunch and a walk in the gardens, and then high tea. In the late afternoon the Royal Family returns to the harbor and the waiting barge ferries everyone back to *Britannia*. There follows a little-known family ceremony that truly marks the start of the royal summer vacation. As *Britannia* steams away, the Queen Mother sets off multicolored rockets from the turrets of her castle for a dramatic farewell, and castle

Castle of Mey

retainers wave white sheets from the battlements. In return, *Britannia* sends up flares, scorching streaks of white light against the evening sky. The excitement over, everyone looks forward to the arrival at Aberdeen, and to those long days to come on the grouse moors of the vast Balmoral estate.

- *Date:* Usually the second Tuesday after the Cowes Regatta, between the 14th and 18th of the month; check with Thurso police.

- *Venue:* Scrabster Harbor, Thurso, Scotland.

- *Getting There:* Thurso is on the very northernmost coast of Scotland and accordingly very hard to reach. *By Car*—The nearest major town is Inverness, about 120 miles to the south by road. From Inverness, take the A9 coast road to Latheron where you head inland along the A895 to Thurso. *By Train*—Thurso has its own little rail line. From London, traveling overnight via Inverness, the journey takes approximately 14 hours.

The Royal Progress to Balmoral

 Usually the royal yacht arrives at Aberdeen harbor at 6:00 A.M. in what is known as "silent order." The engines are cut and *Britannia* docks as quietly as possible so as not to wake the Queen. By early morning a small crowd is waiting to greet the royals, and is often diverted by the sight of a diligent crewman touching up the paintwork—yet again!—on the hull. One year an American tourist saw the Royal Marine band go on deck, and watched open-mouthed as it swung into a lively tune from the musical *The King and I.* "What are they doing that for?" he asked a bearded Scottish photographer, only to be told the band plays every morning before the Queen gets up. "Well," he responded, "that must be the most expensive alarm clock in the world!" Though both men can be forgiven for thinking so, they mistakenly assumed the band was playing to wake the Queen. In fact, it plays for the ceremony of hoisting colors and assembles on the forecastle for the express reason of *not* disturbing Her Majesty, who has her stateroom at the ship's stern.

Long before 10:00, when the royal party departs the royal yacht, the roads to the quayside are lined with hundreds of well-wishers, while on the docks themselves every available space and vantage point has been commandeered. However, the view of the Royal Family is brief, as the royals sweep out of the harbor in a procession of royal cars, so the wise visitor does better to travel instead to Balmoral to watch the Queen review the Guard.

- **Date:** Two days after Scrabster Harbor arrival; usually the local newspapers or the Court and Social column in *The Times* or the *Daily Telegraph* announce a function the Queen is to perform in Aberdeen, which means she will be disembarking from *Britannia* on that day.

- **Venue:** Aberdeen Harbor, Scotland.

- **Getting There:** Aberdeen, on Scotland's east coast, is relatively simple to reach. *By Car*—The city is within easy striking distance of all the major Scottish east coast centers: Edinburgh, Perth, Dundee, Arbroath, and Forfar. *By Train*—Aberdeen is well served by trains from London and other major centers. Overnight from London the journey takes approximately ten hours. *By Air*—There is frequent service from London to Aberdeen airport.

Review of the Guard

 Before the Queen and her family take up residence at Balmoral, she first reviews the Guard of Honor—a Scottish regiment who make a stirring sight in their tartan kilts and furry sporrans. The Queen is usually accompanied by other members of the Royal Family. In one recent year Prince Andrew, in particular, was very much taken by the sight of a kilted soldier with tattoos on his knees.

The occasion provides visitors with their last definite sighting of the Queen and the rest of the family before they start their well-deserved Highland holiday.

- **Date:** Same day as disembarkation from the royal yacht *Britannia* at Aberdeen Harbor (see previous entry).

- **Venue:** Balmoral Castle, Scotland.

- **Getting There:** By Car—take the A93 from Aberdeen to Balmoral, about 50 miles distant.

Crathie Church Service

 As at Sandringham and Windsor, the Queen and the rest of the Royal Family always attend church on Sunday morning when staying at Balmoral. The routine at Crathie is much the same, as thousands of visitors flock to the tiny church to catch a glimpse of the royals in their Sunday finery. The service starts promptly at

11:00, but, unlike that at Sandringham, is not relayed by loud-speaker to the public. On the first Sunday in September the royal party is usually accompanied by the Prime Minister, who is a guest over the weekend.

Just before the service is to begin, the royal party slowly drives the 800 yards from the castle gates along a tree-lined avenue to the small stone church. The Queen, the Duke of Edinburgh, and Prince Edward are normally in the first car, the Prince and Princess of Wales and the Duke and Duchess of York follow in the second, and the third is usually occupied by the Queen Mother and Princess Margaret and her children. The best vantage point is on the private road leading to the church precincts; the nearer the church doorway, the better and longer your view, so get there early.

- **Dates and Times:** Sunday mornings at 11:00 during the Royal Family's residence at Balmoral in August, September, and October.

- **Venue:** Crathie Church, Balmoral Castle, Scotland.

- **Getting There:** Eight miles west of Ballater on A93.

Gatcombe Park Horse Trials

The beauty of these trials is that they are held, quite literally, in Princess Anne's front garden. The show has only been running a few years, but the royal cachet has given them great popularity among both riders and spectators. This is the only time of year when a visitor can see the home of Princess Anne and her family, and watch the comings and goings from her front door. In the past the Princess has been spotted dressed in jeans, rubber boots, the ever-present scarf around her hair, carrying potted fir trees to decorate the show jumping arena, swinging a sledgehammer to knock in a fence post, and even digging a trench to help with drainage during one wet weekend.

Many other members of the Royal Family are apt to drop in. Prince and Princess Michael of Kent are regular visitors, as is Prince Edward. Prince Charles and his wife have been known to pop by for an hour or two. On the second day of the horse trials the astonished royal watcher might even see the royals taking part in a boisterous Land Rover race, speeding about the course collecting time penalties as they go—definitely not the sort of thing you'd be likely to see at a Buckingham Palace garden party!

- *Dates:* Second weekend in the month.

- *Venue:* Gatcombe Park, Minchinhampton, Gloucestershire.

- *Getting There:* Gatcombe Park lies between Minchinhampton and Avening. Coming from either Stroud or Cirencester on the A419, the house will be signposted.

Horse Trials

August is the busiest time of the horse trials calendar. The three listed here are regularly attended by Princess Anne and Captain Mark Phillips. They visit them in sequence, stopping off en route to Scotland from Gloucestershire with their specially constructed horse box.

Dauntsey Park
This is a fairly small horse trial, set among the rolling hills of Wiltshire in the West Country.

- *Dates:* August 1–2.

- *Venue:* Brook Farm, Great Somerset, Chippenham, Wiltshire.

- *Getting There:* Dauntsey Park lies between the little villages of Great and Little Somerset. It is signposted from the M4, however, and can be reached from either exit 16 or 17.

Locko Park
A prestigious horse trials, this is the British Championship, an event of great significance in the horse trials calendar.

- *Dates:* First weekend of the month.

- *Venue:* Locko Park, Spondon, near Derby, Derbyshire.

- *Getting There:* Locko Park lies on the A52, the main Derby-to-Nottingham road; it is well signposted.

Blair Castle
Set among the wild hills of Perthshire, these are perhaps the most spectacular horse trials in Britain, at least as far as setting goes.

- *Date:* Last Sunday of the month.

- *Venue:* Blair Castle, Blair Atholl, Perthshire.

- *Getting There:* Blair Atholl is 25 miles north of Perth on the A9.

SEPTEMBER

September, for all the approaching chill of the fall, is frequently one of the most beautiful times of the year in Britain. And of no part of the country is this more true than Scotland. Often basking in the heat of an Indian summer, with brilliant skies and dazzling sunsets, the Royal Family continue their Balmoral vacation. Their days are spent tramping over the vast, heather-strewn estate, grouse shooting, fishing, or enjoying picnics and barbecues, presided over by the genial Prince Philip.

Back in England, the more equestrian-minded members of the family can be seen in the folksy settings of country horse trials.

Braemar Gathering

 The Braemar Highland games combine the best of Scottish sporting tradition with a chance to see the Royal Family in a relaxed and informal setting. Little wonder, then, that the games, which started in 1817, today attract as many as 20,000 visitors, who come "o'er the hills" to watch the races, shot putting, tug of war matches, and "tossing the caber"—best described as contests between burly Scotsmen to see who can heave a bit of wood the approximate size of a telephone pole the greatest distance. In addition to these sporting entertainments, spectators are also treated to massed pipe band melodies, mournful and rollicking by turns, the whole against the superb mountainous scenery.

Clad in tartan kilts and other suitably Scottish attire, the Royal Family and its Balmoral house guests usually arrive on the scene around 3:00 in the afternoon in their gleaming limousines, to be greeted by games officials and young Highland dancers holding posies of white heather. These are saved to form the center-piece on the Queen's dining table at Balmoral that evening. A wooden cabin decorated with Highland heather is set aside for the royals, and it is from here that they watch the Highland sword dance—not nearly as death-defying as it sounds—the 80 meters race, the tug of war final, and the children's sack race. After presenting the prizes, the Queen and the rest of the family leave the games to head back to Balmoral, having first driven slowly around the grassy track while cheered on by the crowds.

One final tip: If you take A93 (the Ballater-to-Braemar road)

Highland Games

to get to the games, keep a sharp watch on the riverbank. A sudden movement or the noise of a distant Land Rover will often reveal the Princess of Wales out for a walk with her two sons, or Prince Charles salmon fishing in the river Dee. It was here that the very first pictures of the Prince of Wales and the former Lady Diana Spencer were taken. It is not advisable to stop on the roadside, however, since it is constantly patrolled by watchful police; those who linger are liable to be asked to move on.

- **Date:** First Saturday in the month.

- **Venue:** Highland Gathering Arena (half a mile west of Braemar).

- **Getting There:** By Car—from Aberdeen take the A93 to Ballater and then on to Braemar. From Dundee take the A923 to Rattray, then the A93 to Braemar.

Burghley Horse Trials

This is yet another country show where the dedicated watcher can often be rewarded with the sight of Princess Anne and her husband, Captain Mark Phillips—both regulars.

- **Dates:** Second Thursday, Friday, Saturday, and Sunday of the month.

- **Venue:** Burghley House, Stamford, Lincolnshire.

- **Getting There:** By Car—Stamford lies on the A1, 15 miles north of Peterborough. By Train—There is a direct rail link from London.

Tetbury Horse Trials

As this horsy event is just eight miles from Gatcombe Park, home of Princess Anne and her family, it's a pretty sure bet that they will be taking part in this two-day trials. Visitors can also occasionally catch a glimpse of the Prince and Princess of Wales, though rather more likely is the appearance of the Michaels of Kent, who also live in the area.

- **Dates:** Third weekend of the month.

- **Venue:** Church Farm, Long Newton, Tetbury, Gloucestershire.

- **Getting There:** Long Newnton is a mile or so southeast of Tetbury and about 10 miles south of Cirencester on the B4014.

OCTOBER_____

The long Balmoral vacation, started in August, is now coming to an end, and members of the Royal Family reluctantly turn back to work. October is when they start planning their diaries for the months to come, which means accepting and rejecting literally hundreds of invitations. It is a chore which Prince Charles especially abhors. "I hate planning my life so far ahead," he is fond of complaining. This is the month, too, which sees the last country horse trials of the year.

Chatsworth Horse Trials

 The setting for this particular horse trials is the superb estate of Chatsworth, in Derbyshire, ancestral home of the Duke of Devonshire. Even without the royal presence (which is, as usual, provided by Princess Anne and Captain Mark Phillips, and occasionally Princess Michael), this event is intriguing and well worth taking in, as Chatsworth itself is one of Britain's most striking and famous stately homes. So, if by this point you've had it up to the teeth with horses, go simply for the house and the wonderfully landscaped grounds.

- *Dates:* First Thursday to Sunday of the month.

- *Venue:* Chatsworth House, Bakewell, Derbyshire (tel. 024688–2204).

- *Getting There: By Car*—Chatsworth is half a mile east of the village of Edensor on the A623 and four miles east of Bakewell. It is 16 miles from exit 29 of the M1.

The Horse of the Year Show

 The Horse of the Year Show marks the end of the equestrian season. The show normally has the favorite winners of past years, performing in four national jumping classes. The five-day show is usually attended by some member of the Royal Family (not necessarily Princess Anne), although the exact details vary from year to year. Check the Court and Social columns of *The Times,* the *Independent,* the *Star,* and the *Daily Telegraph* during the week.

- *Dates:* October 5–10.

Horse of the Year Show

- **Venue:** Wembley Arena, London.
- **Getting There:** By Tube—Wembley Park.

Crathie Sale of Work

Not many homey church bazaars can boast of having the Queen and the Queen Mother as regular patrons, but that's just what happens at the Crathie Sale of Work. Organized by the local Women's Institute, the bazaar features the familiar tables laden with home-produced cakes, jams, embroidery, and the like, though possibly it is a bit more zealously attended than other church sales. The Queen and her mother always make a point to stop by, and come away with a pot of honey or chocolates for the grandchildren, as well as bouquets of flowers pressed on them by well-wishers. This is a lovely, intimate affair, and little known outside the area; visitors are likely to get a very good view of the royal ladies entering and leaving the church hall.

- **Date:** Second Saturday in the month.
- **Venue:** Crathie Church Hall, Balmoral, Scotland.
- **Getting There:** See "Crathie Church Service" in *September.*

NOVEMBER

With the State Opening of Parliament, the national pulse beats a little faster, newspaper headlines become more sensational, and holiday brochures featuring fun in the sun are ever more alluring. The Royal Family is out in force around the country, opening factories, visiting hospitals, and making speeches. The majority of royal engagements are, therefore, best noted daily in the Court and Social columns of *The Times,* the *Daily Telegraph,* the *Independent,* and the *Star.* But there are several annual events this month which continue to hold the national attention, most notably the Remembrance celebrations, in honor of those who served their country in World Wars I and II, and, most importantly, the State Opening of Parliament.

State Opening of Parliament

 In one of the most important and colorful ceremonies of the royal year, Monarchy meets Democracy in the annual State Opening of Parliament. To underline the essential subservience of the modern monarchy to the wishes of Parliament, the Queen is required to read a speech written for her by the Prime Minister, without altering a single word or syllable. The speech outlines the legislation to be introduced in the coming year by her Government, and the event itself is a perfect example of a constitutional monarchy at work.

Since 1681 all Parliaments have been summoned to meet their sovereign at the Palace of Westminster. On the evening before the State Opening, the royal regalia—the Crown Jewels —held at the Tower of London are brought to Buckingham Palace, and, on the following morning, precede the Queen to Parliament. They are carried in Queen Alexandra's State Coach, the interior of which is lit so that spectators lining the route can clearly see the Imperial State Crown, the Cap of Maintenance, the Sword of State, and the maces of the sergeants at arms.

The Queen, who is usually accompanied by the Princess of

Wales and other members of the family, including the Duke of Edinburgh and the Prince of Wales, leaves Buckingham Palace in a glorious procession of coaches and mounted guards. Her Majesty usually travels in the Irish State Coach, preceded by other coaches carrying various members of the royal household. She is escorted by the mounted Household Cavalry, and the entire route is lined by troops, all the way from Buckingham Palace to the Mall and Horse Guards Parade, through Horse Guards Arch into Whitehall, then to Parliament Square and on into Old Palace Yard and the Houses of Parliament.

Spectators can watch from any position in Whitehall and the Mall, though for a good position nearer to the Houses of Parliament it's best to arrive well before 9:00 A.M. The Old Palace Yard itself is kept clear of onlookers, except for Westminster School students, who exercise a longstanding tradition of watching from the pavement opposite the Soverign's Entrance under the Victoria Tower (the large tower at the opposite end of the Palace of Westminster from the more famous Big Ben).

Stationed to greet the Queen at the Sovereign's Entrance are the Lord Great Chamberlain and the Earl Marshall of England. Meanwhile, in a ceremony which is more than a bit antiquated yet nonetheless carried out to the letter, the Lord Chamberlain, head of the royal household—not to be confused with the Lord Great Chamberlain—is commanded to remain in Buckingham Palace while the sovereign is in Parliament, as a "hostage" for her safe return. When Lord MacLean was Lord Chamberlain, the Queen always greeted him with the same words when returning from a State Opening: "Minded the store well, Chips?"

Once inside Parliament, the Queen is guided to the Robing Room, past a guard of honor of dismounted troopers carrying sabers. Here her ladies-in-waiting dress the monarch in the Crimson Robe of State originally made for Queen Victoria. Its 18-foot train must be supported by no less than four pages of honor, usually the sons or grandsons of senior members of the household. Just before the Queen enters Parliament, however, the royal standard, which flies wherever the Queen is present, is unfurled on the mast 400 feet up on the Victoria Tower, while in Hyde Park and at the Tower of London simultaneous gun salutes are fired by the Royal Artillery.

After the Imperial State Crown has been placed on the Queen's head, a fanfare is sounded, the doors to the royal

Irish State Coach

gallery are opened, and the royal procession moves majestically towards the chamber of the House of Lords. For over 30 years this part of the ceremony has been televised, enabling viewers to delight in the spectacle of the Lord Great Chamberlain maintaining his dignity as he shuffles backwards while holding aloft his white wand in front of the Queen.

As the procession enters the Lords chamber, the lights on the chandeliers are turned up to shine on the splendid assembly of peers in their parliamentary robes of scarlet trimmed with ermine, their wives in long gowns and a scattering of diamond tiaras, the bishops and archbishops in their ample ecclesiastical finery, the judges robed and bewigged, and finally members of the diplomatic corps wearing seemingly every decoration their respective countries have to offer. The peers and peeresses rise, bowing and curtsying to the Queen. On reaching the throne she turns and bids them, "Pray be seated."

The Queen sits on the left-hand throne, the Duke of Edinburgh on the right. Prince Charles and Princess Anne sit one step below their parents on chairs of state, while the Princess of Wales sits next to her husband.

The reason the ceremony of the State Opening of Parliament takes place in the House of Lords rather than in the House of Commons dates back to the days of the long and bloody Civil War in the seventeenth century. Since that time the reigning sovereign has had no physical connection with the House of Commons; and no King or Queen has been allowed to enter the Commons since the days of Charles I. In order to hear the Queen's speech, therefore, Members of Parliament (of the House of Commons, that is) are summoned by an official ominously known as Black Rod, who marches in procession to the Commons from the House of Lords, clad in a uniform of black frock coat, lace collar, silk stockings, and buckled shoes.

The door of the Commons is symbolically shut in his face, however, and he must knock three times with his staff of office before it is opened. He then delivers the message from the Queen, "commanding this honorable house to attend her immediately in the House of Peers." The Speaker of the House is the first to leave, followed by the Prime Minister and the Leader of the Opposition, and then members of both sides of the House. They walk slowly to the Lords, where they are allowed only as far as the bar of the House—which means that very few of them can actually get inside and hear the Queen as she delivers the speech, which is nonetheless ferociously debated later on the floor of the House of Commons.

Once the speech has been read, the Queen returns to the Robing Room, where her ladies-in-waiting help her to remove the Imperial State Crown and her royal robes. She is then taken to the Sovereign's Entrance for the return to Buckingham Palace.

Although an elaborate ritual, the State Opening of Parliament is one of the shorter royal occasions, lasting no more than an hour.

- **Date and Time:** First week in November; the actual day and time are announced in the Court and Social columns of *The Times,* the *Telegraph,* the *Independent,* and the *Star.*

- **Venue:** Houses of Parliament, London, SWI.

- **Getting There:** *By Tube*—Westminster Station is closest to the Houses of Parliament, though Green Park and St. James's stations are also near to Buckingham Palace and the Mall.

- **How to See:** Admission to the opening is by invitation only, so watching the processions to and from the Palace of Westminster is as much as the public ever gets to see of the ceremony, except, of course, by watching television coverage. The way is usually thronged with spectators long in advance, so arrive early.

Festival of Remembrance

 The Royal British Legion's annual Festival of Remembrance at the Royal Albert Hall—a service of commemoration for the dead of two world wars—always draws a large royal turnout. The first festival was held in 1923, just two years after the founding of the British Legion, the country's major war veterans' association. The two-hour festival first features a "muster," when representatives of the armed forces, veterans, and reservists from the Territorial Army all march into the arena. There follow a gymnastics display and, finally, the service of remembrance itself, during which a two-minute silence is observed while a cascade of poppy petals rains from the roof of the hall.

There are actually two performances given, one in the afternoon and another in the evening. The Royal Family will always attend the latter, however, to watch the proceedings from the grand heights of the royal box.

- **Date and Time:** The Saturday before Remembrance Day (the Sunday nearest November 11—the date of the signing of the Armistice to end World War I).

- **Venue:** Royal Albert Hall, London.

- **Getting There:** By Tube—High Street Kensington.

- **Getting In:** Admission by tickets only, available on a first-come, first-served basis from the Box Office, Royal Albert Hall, Kensington Gore, London SW7

Remembrance Sunday

 The Remembrance Day ceremony and parade is one of the most moving and emotional occasions of the royal year, recalling those brave men and women who served and died in the World Wars. The Cenotaph memorial in Whitehall is the focal point of this sober ceremony, and for once political differences are set aside as the Prime Minister, the Leader of the Opposition, cabinet ministers, and politicians of every party assemble before the lofty obelisk.

The Queen herself, accompanied by the royal princes and the royal dukes, stands in silent tribute as the clock strikes 11:00, a moment chosen to mark the signing of the Armistice at the eleventh hour of the eleventh day of the eleventh month in 1918. After the clock has ceased striking and two minutes of silence have been observed, Her Majesty places a wreath of poppies next to the Cenotaph. She is followed by the male members of the Royal Family. Meanwhile, the royal ladies watch from a balcony overlooking Whitehall as a short service is conducted by the Bishop of London, also Dean of the Chapels Royal.

After the laying of the wreaths there is a slow march past the Cenotaph by the men and women of Britain and the Commonwealth, a stirring sight as soldiers present, past, and, some would say, forgotten, proudly wear medals won for gallantries in campaigns, some of whose names are now barely remembered.

The public can watch the ceremony from the pavements of Whitehall, but, as with all major royal events, it is essential to arrive early to be assured of a good position. The parade is televised every year. Though some consider the event an anachronism, the Queen insists on being present; and from the number of people who turn out to watch, its popularity and place in the royal year show no danger of diminishing.

- **Date and Time:** Sunday closest to November 11 (date of the signing of the Armistice to end World War I) at 11:00 A.M.

- **Venue:** Cenotaph, Whitehall, London SW1.

- **Getting There:** By Tube—Westminster, Charing Cross.

- **How to See:** No tickets are necessary, but an early arrival is mandatory if you wish to see anything at all.

DECEMBER

Traditionally a time for family and friends as thoughts turn towards Christmas, December sees the children as a natural focus of attention. This parental sentiment is echoed by the Royal Family, though the royal children are treated with quite a bit more privilege than the rest of us ever were. Harrod's—that *grande dame* of department stores—opens specially for the Princess of Wales and her two small sons, so that Prince William and Prince Harry can have a private visit with Santa Claus.

Christmas itself comes not once but twice a year for the Queen and her family. The first celebration is the traditional one on December 25, when the Royal Family is gathered at Windsor Castle. The second Christmas is celebrated at Sandringham so that staff who work in the Queen's Norfolk home are not disappointed. Another slightly unusual custom, and one dating back to Queen Alexandra, the wife of Edward VII, has the family opening its presents on Christmas Eve rather than on Christmas Day. By the early afternoon of Christmas Eve, there is a marvelous air of anticipation and hustle bustle as the final preparations are made by the staff for the Royal Family. However, the real reason for Christmas is not forgotten, and this gives the public a chance to see the Royal Family during the festive season.

Christmas Eve Service at Windsor

A Christmas Eve service is held at midnight in the lower ward of the magnificent St. George's Chapel, which several members of the Royal Family will walk down the hill to attend. Princess Margaret and the Duchess of Kent, in particular, almost always mingle

111

with the public who have waited patiently to celebrate this special time of year with the royals.

- **Date and Time:** December 24, at midnight.

- **Venue:** St. George's Chapel, Windsor Castle, Windsor, Royal Berkshire.

- **Getting There:** See "Easter at Windsor" in *April.*

Christmas Day at Windsor

 Christmas represents the single time of year when every member of the Royal Family stays at Windsor Castle, with no exceptions. What with all the Windsors, Gloucesters, and Kents floating around, Windsor Castle, large as it is, is soon filled to bursting point. Some 35 sat down to Christmas lunch recently, and it is rumored that the Queen is seriously considering inviting only the immediate members of the Royal Family to Christmas with her at Windsor.

At 11:00 A.M. sharp, members of the Royal Family arrive in cars at St. George's Chapel—it's often too cold for them to manage the five-minute walk—to be greeted by the dean. After the hour-long service, the royals emerge from the church and head to the vestry for a Christmas drink with the local clergy. This particular bit of Christmas cheer usually lasts about 20 minutes, whereupon they re-emerge to the greetings and good wishes of the waiting crowd. Then they climb back into their limousines, and on their return to the castle they give a final wave to the well-wishers before disappearing inside to await Christmas Day lunch.

Once back from the service the elder royals will drop in to the nursery to see the children, who always have their Christmas lunch at 12:45. The Queen's lunch is held at 1:15, and its menu is entirely traditional—lobster soup to start, then roast turkey and roast potatoes, and a flaming Christmas pudding with brandy sauce. Lunch is over by 3 o'clock so that—along with the rest of the nation—everyone can settle down to watch the Queen's speech on television. After that, the family usually goes for a short walk to offset the effects of the huge feast; but soon it's followed by tea, and then a light supper at 8:15—if anyone is still hungry, that is.

Boxing Day, the day after Christmas, is set aside for shooting, unless it happens to fall on a Sunday. That evening the royals gather in the Garter Throne Room and watch a movie which will have been specially lent by a film company. Then, after another day's shooting, the entire Court moves on to Sandringham for another Christmas celebration and the start of another royal year.

- *Date and Time:* December 25 at 11:00.

- *Venue:* St. George's Chapel, Windsor Castle, Royal Berkshire.

- *Getting There:* See above.

ROYAL RESIDENCES

ROYAL PALACES

Buckingham Palace

Buckingham Palace is probably the most famous palace in the world, its great gray facade as much a symbol of Britain and the Royal Family as the cool, Classical exterior of the White House is of America and the Presidency. It also enjoys the distinction of being one of the most photographed buildings in the world. Yet for all its familiarity and fame, it is an intensely discreet place. Few who have snapped its imposing Edwardian exterior or the scarlet-coated guardsmen outside it have ever ventured inside.

To most Britons it's simply "the palace." This is the nerve center of the Royal Family, its High Command, the monarch's official London residence. It is from here that the Queen's affairs are arranged, her complex schedule planned. And it is here that so much of the formality and grandeur of royalty is played out, where investitures, state banquets, and receptions are held, and the famous summer garden parties given, when the streets around the palace are blocked solid as bigwigs of all descriptions arrive for a cup of tea and the chance of a chat with their sovereign. It is to Buckingham Palace that the Queen and her family return after all the major state occasions—the arrival of a foreign dignitary, the Trooping of the Color, the State Opening of Parliament, a royal wedding—to stand on the second-floor balcony and wave to the assembled multitudes.

Yet despite, or very possibly because of, its rigid and courtly formality, the Queen has never felt much affection for Buckingham Palace. On the death of her father in 1952, she and Prince Philip suggested quite seriously that they be allowed to continue to live in nearby and much smaller Clarence House. Her grandfather George V seems to have had even less liking for it, and considered pulling it down. But, as ever with the Windsors, duty prevailed, and indeed prevails, as the gorgeous royal standard, flying over the facade of the palace whenever the Queen is home, makes very clear.

It is a key characteristic of the Royal Family, a central article of faith, that its affairs always be beautifully ordered and organized. When the Queen's schedule says she will arrive at 11:00, she arrives at 11:00, prompt. This legendary reliability is reflect-

Buckingham Palace

ed in the dignified atmosphere of the palace. Here, trusted courtiers work out the details of the monarch's affairs in a time-honored atmosphere of calm efficiency. Urbane good manners are *de rigeur.* Once, the story runs, a private secretary was stopped by a visitor. The official listened patiently to the man and offered a few words of advice before glancing at his watch and saying calmly, "I'm sorry, I must leave you. My house is on fire."

Yet aside from its function as royal office building and ceremonial headquarters, Buckingham Palace is still a family home. Visitors are frequently amazed at the number of toys cluttering its miles of red-carpeted corridors, those same corridors along which the Queen will proceed in full regal majesty en route to a State banquet, and, yes, those same corridors along which Princess Diana reputedly rollerskated wearing headphones.

On one occasion a secretary was astonished to see the Queen running headlong down one of the corridors in pursuit of a fleeing Prince William. Catching the renegade young Prince, she spotted the secretary and explained, "That's the trouble with this place. There are too many corridors." Then she added with a smile, "Don't worry, young lady. This will happen to you one day."

Buckingham Palace, originally Buckingham House, takes its name from the Duke of Buckingham, for whom it was built in the early eighteenth century. Though a substantial house, it was then very much smaller than today's lordly edifice. In 1762 it was bought by George III. A stolid, rather pedestrian king, never happier than when among his collection of watches and clocks, George III did little to the building, preferring the domestic delights of his little house at Kew to the formality of Buckingham Palace. His son George IV was a man—and King—of very different temperament, a reckless spendthrift and frantic setter of fashion. Yet he had a superb eye for all things artistic and a strong sense of what was fitting for the King of England. He commissioned John Nash to rebuild the palace in a more appropriately regal style. Much of its most splendid architecture is the work of Nash, especially the fine garden front. In 1847 Queen Victoria and Prince Albert added, among much else, the east wing, which became the front facade. This in turn was remodeled in the years before World War I by Aston Webb, a capable but dull architect. Webb also put up the grandiose Queen Victoria Memorial in front of the palace, and remodeled the Mall, the grand ceremonial boulevard that stretches away from the palace to Admiralty Arch and Trafalgar Square. Thus, though Buckingham Palace remains essentially an eighteenth- and nineteenth-century building, it is these Edwardian additions that form the popular view of the palace; indeed, really the only view for the thronging masses outside.

But Buckingham Palace does boast the most famous and regular tourist show in London, though it is one with no royal participation. The Changing of the Guard takes place every day from April through July—and every other day from August through March—at 11:00. It's an impressive sight, as the guardsmen in their distinctive busbies—huge fur hats—march in from their barracks around the corner in Birdcage Walk, bands playing and flags flying. But get there early if you want a decent view.

The palace's principal rooms, the state rooms, are all on the second floor, reached by a magnificent marble staircase. They consist of the Throne Room, graced by seven dazzling chandeliers; the Ballroom; the State Dining Room (the banquets given here are so complex that traffic lights have been installed outside to tell servants when to enter with the next course); the Music Room, where royal christenings normally take place; the White Drawing Room, where the Royal Family assembles on state occasions before proceeding to the Ballroom; and finally the Blue Drawing Room, often claimed to be the most beautiful room in the palace. As if this was not enough, the west wing is one immense picture gallery, 155 feet long. Both the Queen and Prince Philip have suites on this floor, as well as their own offices. The majority of the other offices in the building are on the first floor.

All the other family bedrooms, and all the staff bedrooms, are on the third floor. Both Prince Edward and Princess Anne have suites here. Until his marriage to Sarah Ferguson in 1986, Prince Andrew, the Duke of York, had rooms in the old nursery, converted by him into bachelor quarters. Today, he and the Duchess live in Prince Charles's old rooms.

One of the great glories of the palace is its gardens, some 40 acres of prime real estate in the very heart of London. Lucky guests at one of the regular summer garden parties (to which you must, naturally, be invited, which is fortunate if you're an Admiral of the Fleet or a bishop but hard on the rest of the common herd) are among the select few who ever get to see the luscious expanse. You can, it's true, get a glimpse of the ponds, walks, lawns, trees, and serried ranks of flowers—even of the royal tennis courts—from the top of a red London bus, but that's about as close as most people are ever likely to get to the Queen's green acres. There was a time when the great brick wall round the gardens could be easily scaled, allowing at least a peek over them. Three young German tourists went even further one hot summer evening. Thinking they had reached nearby Hyde Park, they shinnied over the walls and settled down for the night. They were discovered the next morning by some very startled gardeners. Security was tightened considerably, but not enough to prevent another surprise early-morning call a year or so later. But this time it was the Queen herself who was awakened. Early one day in July 1982, Michael Fagan, unemployed and mentally disturbed, broke into the palace and found his way to the Queen's bedroom. There he engaged his surprised but collected sovereign in a rambling 25-minute discourse on his broken marriage. There were red faces all round after this. Security was stepped up once more. Today, cameras, spiked railings, and patrolling policemen are much in evidence.

Still, even though for most people, Londoners and tourists alike, Buckingham Palace maintains its discreet distance, highly visible but remote, there are at least two parts of the building that can be visited. These are the Royal Mews and the Queen's Gallery, both along the south side of the palace on Buckingham Palace Road. The gallery, housed in what was originally the private chapel, the most severely bombed part of the building in the war, is one of the rare places where exhibitions of the Queen's fabulous collection of pictures are put on. Though owned by the Queen, they are essentially held in trust by her and cannot be resold.

In the Royal Mews, amid the pomp of John Nash's grandiose stables, can be seen many of the state coaches, including the superb State Carriage itself, an immensely elaborate gilded affair built in 1761. This was the carriage used in the Queen's coronation.

- **Address:** Buckingham Palace, The Mall, London SW1.

- **Getting There:** Tubes—Green Park, St. James's Park, Victoria.

- **Changing of the Guard:** April through July, daily at 11:00; August through March, alternate days at 11:00. State occasions and wet weather can lead to cancellation.

- *Queen's Gallery:* Tel. 930 4832. Open Tues. to Sat. 11–5, Sun. 2–5; closed Mon. Admission £1.10, children and senior citizens 50p.

- *The Royal Mews:* Open Wed. and Thurs. only, 2–4; closed Ascot Week and state occasions.

Kensington Palace

Kensington Palace, standing at the west end of Kensington Gardens about two miles from Buckingham Palace, is one of the most extraordinary of the royal palaces. For the dedicated royalty watcher it can rank high among the list of top spots.

This might seem a rash statement, for there are no unforgettable sights here, no great formal occasions. Even the building itself seems modest; more a plain country home than a grand royal palace. There are no scarlet-coated guardsmen outside. Security seems deceptively absent. You can walk right up to the building, and large parts of it are open to the public. Yet within its orange brick walls live no less than 14 members of the Royal Family. From the outside, it seems hard to believe that they could all squeeze in: Prince Charles and Princess Diana, plus the Princes William and Harry; Princess Margaret; the Duke and Duchess of Gloucester, plus their three children; and Prince and Princess Michael of Kent, plus their two children. In addition, a number of the outbuildings, much as at Hampton Court and St. James's Palace, have been turned into "grace and favor" apartments, where senior courtiers and other retired royal servants see out their days rent free, courtesy of a grateful sovereign.

The building passed into royal hands in 1689. It was bought by William of Orange, Dutch-born and dourly Protestant new King of England. He found that the fogs and mists from the Thames at Whitehall Palace, then the royal residence, aggravated his asthma. Moreover, the rural setting of Kensington Palace and its small size were much more to his simple taste than the ungainly Tudor grandeur of Whitehall. Even today, despite many additions and extensions by Wren, Vanbrugh, Hawksmoor, and others, Kensington Palace retains its domestic, rather homey quality. Its setting in Kensington Gardens, themselves largely developed by Queen Anne, William's successor, contribute greatly to this sense of rural simplicity.

Kensington Palace

Once George II bought Buckingham Place, Kensington Palace passed out of royal favor, though it remained royal property. By the nineteenth century, it was famous only as the birthplace of Queens Victoria and Mary, and as the unlikely setting, in 1837, for a new dawn in English history when the eighteen-year-old Princess Victoria was summoned from her bed to be told of the death of her uncle, William IV, and her accession to the throne.

In recent times the palace has developed a new lease on life as members of the burgeoning Royal Family have had to find beds for themselves in London. Hence the ever growing number of royals here, and the discreet iron grip of security in which it is clasped.

For the royalty watcher, the draw here is twofold. First, you can visit the state apartments, a series of elegant Baroque paneled rooms, with views over the park, a collection of court costumes, and much fine decoration, including a handsome painted staircase and the pretty little room where Queen Victoria was born. Second, there's the added attraction of spotting the royals. This is really only for the dedicated. There's no guarantee of seeing anyone, but if you stand outside the main entrance—the entrance facing *away* from the park—you may see Prince Charles and Princess Diana on their way to or from one of their numerous appointments, or Prince William being taken to school by his detective. You may also spy Princess Michael hurrying off to her publishers or to decorate a house; or perhaps a suntanned Princess Margaret returning home from another jaunt to the Caribbean. Even the comings and goings of delivery trucks and royal courtiers can give a fascinating insight into the daily routines of the royal folk who live within these walls. For more information, see "February" in *The Royal Year.*

- *Address:* Kensington Palace, Kensington Gardens, London W8.

- *Getting There: Tubes*—High Street Kensington, Notting Hill Gate, Queensway.

- *State Apartments and Court Dress Collection:* Tel. 937 9561. Open Mon. to Sat. 11–5, Mon. to Fri. 11–6 during temporary exhibits; closed Sun. Admission free.

St. James's Palace

St. James's Palace, facing the Mall and bordering Clarence House, is perhaps the prettiest—certainly it's the most atmospheric—of London's royal palaces. Sadly, despite its nominal role as metropolitan home of the monarch and its brilliant guardsmen standing sentinel outside, it is today much reduced in royal importance.

The accession of every new sovereign is, it's true, proclaimed here. And foreign ambassadors to Britain are officially accredited to the Court of St. James's. But tellingly, when they are received formally by the Queen, it is Buckingham Palace they visit.

St. James's Palace stands on the site of a hospital built around 1100. Henry VIII bought the hospital in 1531 and immediately tore it down to build a hunting lodge. (St. James's Park opposite was once part of an extensive royal hunting preserve.) The Tudor monarch then quickly extended the building, though today only the sturdy gatehouse and parts of the beautiful Chapel Royal remain from this period.

The palace grew rapidly in importance following the terrible fire in 1698 which all but obliterated nearby Whitehall Palace.

In the nineteenth century it was much extended and improved by those incorrigible improvers and builders, George IV and John Nash.

Today the palace is occupied by a number of royal officials, the Lord Chamberlain among them. Other parts of the building have been given over to "grace and favor" apartments.

It is not usually possible to visit St. James's Palace, though you may walk quite freely around a number of its beautiful court-yards. But on a small number of special royal occasions it is sometimes possible to visit the Chapel Royal. Here, under a ceiling designed by Holbein, several royal marriages have taken place, including that of Queen Victoria and Prince Albert in 1840 and the future George V in 1893.

- *Address:* St. James's Palace, Clarence Row, Pall Mall, London SW1.

- *Getting There: Tube*—Green Park.

Windsor Castle

Windsor, 25 miles west of central London, is an essential day out for any visitor to London. The principal attraction is the castle, high on a bluff above the Thames with magnificent views over the surrounding country. The first castle here was built by William the Conqueror in the eleventh century, and was added to by Henry II and Henry III. The town that grew with this great fortification is just as old and interesting, its narrow streets and ancient buildings huddled around the gray stone walls of the castle.

Most medieval kings resided in Windsor. Edward I gave the town its royal charter, while Edward III transformed the old castle, building new apartments, the great Round Tower, the gateway, and the two other towers, all of which still stand today. Edward IV began St. George's Chapel, while Henry VII completed the nave, and Henry VIII set the vault over the choir. Elizabeth I built the north terrace, and Charles II restored the state apartments.

But it was George IV, in the early nineteenth century, who transformed the essentially medieval castle into the royal palace you can visit today. Spending lavishly, he had substantial areas rebuilt, including the Round Tower, whose height was raised by 30 feet in order to improve the view of the castle from afar. He also built the Waterloo Gallery, a sumptuous hall lined with gigantic portraits by Lawrence of the victors of Waterloo.

Windsor Castle

Queen Victoria was singularly fond of Windsor, spending much of her time here, especially after the death of Prince Albert, giving rise to her sobriquet "the widow of Windsor." It was Victoria, too, who built the lavish mausoleum at nearby Frogmore for Albert and herself. The Duke and Duchess of Windsor are buried here, too.

The present Queen uses the castle almost more than any of her predecessors. It has become a sort of handy weekend country retreat, as well as the regular royal rendezvous at Christmas, Easter, and Ascot Week in June.

It is at Windsor more than at any of the royal residences that visitors can fully appreciate the extent of the Queen's wealth of pictures, furniture, and porcelain—all of it housed in buildings of deep historic significance.

In addition to the splendid state apartments, a visit to Queen Mary's Doll's House should not be missed. Given to Queen Mary in 1924, it is a perfect, fully-working palace within a palace. There are electric lights, the doors all have keys, the elevators work, and there is running water. There is even a Lilliputian library, with over 200 tiny books specially written by famous authors.

Architecturally, probably the finest treasure at Windsor is St. George's Chapel. One of the noblest buildings in England, it is over 230 feet long, with two tiers of great windows, and hundreds of gargoyles, buttresses, and pinnacles. Light floods in from the stained-glass windows, and above the dark oak of the stalls hang the banners, swords, and helmets of the Knights of the Order of the Garter. Here lie some of the most famous of England's kings: Henry VI, Henry VIII (Jane Seymour, the mother of his only son, is also here), George III, George IV, William IV, Edward VII, George V, and George VI, father of the present Queen.

The beauty of the church in the Lower Ward is matched by the exquisite reception rooms, a guard room, and a picture gallery. The Gobelin tapestries in the reception rooms are magnificent, as is the picture collection, with a Rubens room and a Van Dyck room. The royal library contains an almost unbelievable wealth of treasures, including a series of priceless Leonardo drawings, and 87 portraits by Holbein.

You can visit the Royal Mews, too. As well as many fascinating carriages and coaches, there's a selection from the hundreds of gifts presented to the Queen the world over. Finally, in the town itself is a waxwork exhibition that focuses on Queen Victoria's Diamond Jubilee in 1897. Called "Royalty and Empire," it successfully recreates the pomp and pageantry of a state occasion.

The parkland surrounding Windsor Castle—Windsor Great Park—is magnificent, its nearly 4,800 rolling acres linked to the castle by the Long Walk, a stately, tree-lined avenue originally planted by Charles II. On the southeast side of the castle is the smaller Home Park, filled with majestic oaks, many of which were planted in the reign of Elizabeth I.

- *Address:* Windsor Castle, Windsor, Royal Berkshire (tel. 0753– 868286).

- *Getting There: By Car*—Take the M4 from London. *By Train*—From Waterloo Station every half-hour; journey time approx. 50 minutes; tel. 928 5100 for train times and fares. *By Bus*—Three Greenline buses an hour from Victoria Coach Station, Eccleston Bridge, London SW1; journey time approx. 60 minutes; tel. 834 6563 for times and fares.

- *Castle Precincts:* Open daily Apr., and Sept. to late Oct., 10–5:15; May through Aug., 10–7:15; and late Oct. through Mar., 10–4:15. Admission free.

- *State Apartments:* Open Mon. to Sat., Jan. through Mar. and late Oct. through Dec., 10:30–3; and Apr. through late Oct., 10:30–5, Sun., open mid-May to mid-Oct., 1:30–5, only. Closed when Queen is in official residence, which times are rather complicated—best to check with the Castle before making a trip by calling the above number. Admission £1.40, children 60p.

- *Queen Mary's Dolls' House, Exhibition of Drawings, and Royal Mews:* Similar times to those of the state apartments, but it's best to call ahead on above number. Admission 60p, children 20p.

- *St. George's Chapel:* May through Oct., Mon. to Sat. 10:45–4, Sun. 2–4. Nov. through Apr., Mon. to Sat. 10:45–3:45, Sun. 2–3:45. Admission £1.30, children 60p.

The Palace of Holyroodhouse

Holyroodhouse in Edinburgh is the monarch's official residence in Scotland. Following the custom established by Queen Victoria, the Queen and her court decamp up here from London for two weeks every summer, usually in late June and early July. Other than for this brief spell, and a short occupation by the Scottish General Assembly at the end of May, Holyroodhouse is open to the public, who are free to explore its magnificent state apartments and fine grounds.

The palace is the very stuff of fairy tales, with great granite turrets and magnificent views in every direction over the stately Scottish capital. Much of the tragic and brutal histories of Mary, Queen of Scots, and the doomed Bonnie Prince Charlie were played out here.

Originally an abbey, built in the twelfth century by King David I as an offering for his deliverance from a rampaging stag above whose antlers a "holy rood" or cross is said to have appeared, the palace stands at the eastern end of the Royal Mile. Around it is Queen's Park—King's Park if a king is on the throne—a public park of springy turf and small lochs. The ruins of the abbey still stand beside the present palace. Here you might be lucky enough to see the Queen's Bodyguard for Scotland practicing with their longbows. They are a corps of elderly and respectable citizens whose appearance in their bizarre uniforms has been likened to that of generals rolled in spinach. An equally ceremonial military occasion, though this time involving the Black Watch, one of the British Army's crack regiments, is the Ceremony of the Keys. It takes place every year in the forecourt of the palace, with the Queen much in evidence, and can easily be seen from the palace railings. For full details see "July" in *The Royal Year.*

The state apartments—rebuilt by Charles II between 1671 and 1677—recall the glamour and violence of Stuart history, especially the little supper room where in 1566 David Rizzio, secretary and lover of Mary, Queen of Scots, was dragged from behind her skirts and stabbed to death. The principal room is the 124-foot-long Picture Gallery, scene of many a wild revel during the brief heyday of Bonnie Prince Charlie. You'll also be shown the Chapel Royal, where many Scottish monarchs were married, and the Royal Vault, where many others were buried among numerous ancient and anonymous graves.

- **Address:** The Palace of Holyroodhouse, Cannongate, Edinburgh, Scotland (tel. 031–556 7371).

- **State and Historical Apartments:** Open April through Oct., Mon. to Sat. 9:30–5:15, Sun. 10:30–4:30; Nov. through Mar., Mon. to Sat. 9:30–3:45.

OTHER ROYAL PALACES
Hampton Court Palace

Hampton Court, built originally in the early sixteenth century by Cardinal Thomas Wolsey, Archbishop of York, taken over by Henry VIII and extended by him, and then extended again at the end of the seventeenth century by William and Mary, is architecturally the finest palace in Britain. A mellow red-brick building, bristling with turrets and twisted chimneys in the very best Tudor tradition, it stands on a loop of the Thames, about twenty miles upstream from London.

Though it is still technically a royal palace, royalty ceased to live here with George III. He, poor man, preferred the seclusion of Kew, where he was finally confined during his madness. Until then, every British monarch from Henry VIII onwards had used the palace. Charles II even spent his honeymoon here. William and Mary especially loved Hampton Court, and much of their

Hampton Court Palace

life-style here is still in evidence, in particular in the marvelous collections of Delftware and other fine porcelain.

Although the Royal Family maintains a close interest in the palace's upkeep—following a serious fire at Easter 1986, the Queen, Prince Philip, and Prince Charles all came quickly to inspect the damage—it is a pity this superb setting is not used more for ceremonial occasions. Today, the most obvious evidence of royalty is the series of grace and favor apartments ranged down one side of the building. (It was in one of these that the fire started, begun when a candle, by which a general's widow had chosen to read, was knocked to the ground.)

The palace remains open year-round, however, and though it may disappoint keen royalty watchers, anyone with a taste for English history and her kings and queens will feel very much at home.

The palace divides itself neatly into two styles: Tudor, and William and Mary. To progress from the Tudor part of the building, with its cobbled courtyards, roundels of Roman emperors, allegorical tapestries, ornate woodwork, and tiny, almost claustrophobic chambers, into the elegant and gracious state apartments, with spacious views over gardens and parks, is to walk through a central part of English history. However, it must be said that some of the rooms are somewhat empty, and that a good number of the paintings are hung so high on the walls that it is virtually impossible to see them. Nonetheless, some rooms are furnished with many excellent pieces, especially the bedrooms, with their fourposter beds surmounted by plumes and rearing like enormous catafalques.

The site beside the slow-moving Thames is idyllic. The old palace itself, steeped in history, hung with priceless paintings, full of echoing corridors and cavernous Tudor kitchens—not to mention a couple of royal ghosts, the luckless shades of Jane Seymour and Catherine Howard, two of Henry's unfortunate queens—is set in a park alive with dappled deer and tall ancestral trees, with magnificent ornamental gardens, an elegant Orangery, and the celebrated maze.

- **Address:** Hampton Court Palace, Hampton Court, East Molesey (tel. 977 8441).

- **Getting There:** By Train—From Waterloo Station every half-hour; journey time approx. 30 minutes; tel. 928 5100 for train times and fares. By Bus—Hourly Greenline buses from Victoria Coach Station, Eccleston Bridge, London SW1; journey time approx. 40 minutes; tel.

129

834 6563 for times and fares. *By Boat*—From Westminster Pier, April through Oct. Four sailings daily; journey time approx. three to four hours; tel. 930 2062 for times and fares.

- **State Apartments:** Open April through Sept., Mon. to Sat. 9:30–6, Sun. 11–6; Oct. through Mar., Mon. to Sat., 9:30–5, Sun. 2–5. Admission £2.20, £2 in winter, children £1.

Kew Palace

Kew Palace is the smallest and the most appealing of the royal palaces. In fact it's really a palace in name only, a palace almost by accident. It stands, trim and domestic, six miles west of central London in the Royal Botanical Gardens at Kew, 300 acres of landscaped public gardens and the country's leading botanical institute.

Ardent royalty spotters will find little to divert them here, but avid gardeners and historians, or just those in search of a delightful day out, will be enchanted.

Kew Palace, originally the Old Dutch House, complete with gables and delicate brickwork, owes its royal role to George III. He had little time for the splendors of court life, and spent much of his life, especially his declining years, in the rural bliss of Kew. At first he and his queen, Charlotte, lived in the White House, known then as Kew Palace. In 1803 they had it demolished, intending to rebuild it on a more lavish scale. While the work progressed, he and Charlotte moved into the Old Dutch House. But as poor George descended slowly into madness, work on the new building first slowed, then halted.

Following George's death in 1820, his son, George IV, ordered the destruction of his father's stillborn palace. But the Old Dutch House, or Kew Palace as it subsequently became, is still there, a charmingly domestic spot, quite unlike a royal building. It has been carefully restored and is a delight to explore. The little formal gardens to its side and rear have been redeveloped as a seventeenth-century herbal garden. With its trim hedges, statuary, formal paths, and carefully laid out plants and flowers, it is engaging.

Visitors to Kew should also take the opportunity to visit the rest of the gardens, especially the splendid nineteenth-century greenhouses—the Palm House and the Temperate House—and the Chinesse Pagoda, an eccentric eighteenth-century work that can be seen for miles around.

- **Address:** Kew Palace, Royal Botanic Gardens, Kew Road, Richmond, Surrey (tel. 940 3321).

- **Getting There:** *Tube*—Kew Gardens. *By Boat*—From Westminster Pier, en route to Hampton Court; see Hampton Court for details.

- **Palace:** Open daily April through Sept., 11–5:30. Admission 80p, under-16s and senior citizens 40p.

The Tower of London

The Tower of London is the most impressive of Britain's royal palaces, a historic and dramatic series of buildings intimately bound to the story of London and Britain's kings and queens. Every monarch from William the Conqueror in the eleventh century to Henry III in the thirteenth century lived here, but practically every other monarch has had some connection with the place. At other times the Tower has been the site of the Royal Mint, home to the Public Records, the Royal Menagerie and the Royal Observatory, and most famously a prison and scene of countless executions. Those who have been incarcerated here include Anne Boleyn (who had previously married Henry VIII in the chapel here), Queen Elizabeth I (before she came to the throne), Sir Walter Raleigh (he spent 13 years here), and Robert Devereux, Earl of Essex and long-time favorite of Elizabeth I. The Little Princes in the Tower, believed to have been murdered by Richard III, are also thought to have met their fate here.

But for many the star attractions at the Tower are the Crown Jewels, a breathtakingly beautiful collection of regalia, precious stones, and silver and gold, much of it priceless. Perhaps the most startling exhibits are the Royal Scepter, containing the largest cut diamond in the world, weighing an astounding 530 carats, and the Imperial State Crown, made for the coronation of Queen Victoria in 1838 and containing some 3,000 precious stones, mainly diamonds and pearls, including the second largest cut diamond in the world. Like that in the Royal Scepter, it was cut from the Cullinan diamond—the Star of Africa. But almost as extraordinary is the immense Koh-i-noor diamond, set in a crown made for the coronation of Queen Elizabeth (now the Queen Mother) in 1937.

The best and most interesting way to see the Tower, at least on a first visit, is to join one of the many free tours given by the Beefeaters—the Constabulary, or Yeoman Warders, of the

Tower of
London

Tower. They wear a distinctive and picturesque black Tudor uniform and, on special occasions, an even more magnificent red uniform. Tours start by the main entrance and leave every 15 minutes or so.

Begun originally by William the Conqueror in 1077, the Tower has been added to and extended numerous times over the centuries. The major points of interest are the White Tower, William's massive, brooding fortress at the heart of the complex; the Bloody Tower, built around 1380 and scene of the murder of the Little Princes, or so the story goes; the little chapel of St. Peter ad Vincula (1520), where the corpses of some 2,000 prisoners, executed in the Tower, were dumped unceremoniously under the flagstones; and the Beauchamp Tower, dating mainly from the reign of Henry VIII and used to house prisoners of importance. It is here in the Beauchamp Tower as much as anywhere in the Tower that the sense of the centuries unfolding is most vivid.

But there is much, much more to see in this richly historic site, where the full pomp, majesty, violence, and brutality of England's story was played out. The Royal Family has come a long way since then.

- **Address:** Tower of London, Tower Hill, EC3 (tel. 709 0765).

- **Getting There:** *Tube*—Tower Hill.

- **The Tower:** Open March through Oct., Mon. to Sat. 9:30–4:45, Sun. 2–5:45; Nov. through Feb., Mon. to Sat. 9:30–4:30, closed Sun. Jewel House closed Feb. Admission £4 (£3 in winter), senior citizens and children £1.50.

PRIVATE ROYAL HOMES
Anmer Hall

The Duke and Duchess of Kent use this fine late-Georgian house on weekends. The house, set in ten acres of the Sandringham estate, has the fourteenth-century Church of St. Mary in its grounds.

Anmer Hall is a private residence and is not open to the public.

Balmoral Castle

Among the multitude of customs and habits inherited by the present Royal Family from Queen Victoria, the annual trip north to Scotland and Balmoral Castle in August and September must be very near the top of the pile. Indeed, until Victoria and Prince Albert bought their "pretty little castle in the old Scottish style" in 1847, no self-respecting monarchs ever went near Scotland if they could possibly help it. But Victoria and Albert, their heads swirling with the romantic tales of Sir Walter Scott, Scotland's most famous propagandist, quickly changed all that. From almost the moment they signed the deeds on the house, Scotland had "arrived."

"Pretty little castle" or not, they lost no time pulling it down and putting up something more substantial. Balmoral has remained something of a shrine to Victoria, though the original decorations, which embraced the Highland tradition whole-heartedly, with stags' heads abounding, furniture made from antlers, tartan carpets and wallpaper, and bagpipes wailing incessantly, have been toned down. (Even the little train that brought distinguished visitors from Ballater eight miles away was decked out with a tartan locomotive.)

Balmoral Castle

Like Sandringham, Balmoral is a private house, owned personally by the Queen and maintained from her own money. But, again like Sandringham, astute management of the enormous estate—with farming, forestry, and shooting well to the fore—has ensured that it is a profitable concern.

It is the combination of privacy and the incomparable beauty of its setting that has helped make Balmoral a treasured retreat of the Royal Family. Asked once what her favorite vacation was, Princess Anne replied, "Two weeks at Balmoral with my family."

It was here that Prince Charles wrote his best-selling children's book, *The Old Man of Lochnagar*, Lochnagar being the 3,800-foot mountain overlooking the estate. A hearty walk up it after a picnic lunch at nearby Loch Muick remains a long-standing family favorite. The purple heather, grazing deer, scudding clouds, pure Deeside air, and rushing Highland streams provide the perfect setting for them to unwind and escape the pressures of their hectic lives. Prince Charles in particular finds Balmoral irresistible, for the privacy it affords him, the chance for a little salmon fishing, and the opportunity to commune gently with the untrammeled beauty of the setting.

Although Balmoral is not generally open to the public, parts of the grounds are open in early summer. An exhibition of nineteenth-century royal life is also held in the ballroom over the same period, allowing visitors a chance to peek at the rest of the interior. See below for full details.

The most likely place to catch a glimpse of the Royal Family is on Sunday mornings at nearby Craithie church, a mile from the castle on the main Braemar road. Members of the family are also occasionally to be seen shopping in Ballater, where almost every other shop sports the "By Royal Appointment" coat of arms, the much prized Royal Warrant.

- *Address:* Balmoral Castle, near Ballater, Grampian, Scotland.

- *Getting There:* Eight miles west of Ballater on A93.

- *House and Grounds:* Open May through July, Mon. to Sat., 10–5. Admission £1.10, children free.

Barnwell Manor

Barnwell Manor, at Barnwell St. Andrew, near Oundle in Northamptonshire, is the country seat of the Duke and Duchess of Gloucester, and the home of the Duke's mother, Princess Alice.

The manor was purchased by the Duke's father, Prince Henry, Duke of Gloucester, in 1935, two years after his marriage to Lady Alice Montagu-Douglas-Scott, daughter of the seventh Duke of Buccleuch. Before that, it had been part of the ancestral estates of the Buccleuchs and their ancestors, the Montagus, since the reign of Henry VIII.

It is a fine house of some 40 rooms, built of local stone with gables and mullioned windows. The Duke has space to devote one room to displays of World War I model soldiers. A path leads directly to the village church, where there are memorials to both the late Duke and his eldest son, Prince William, who was killed in a flying accident in 1972.

Barnwell Manor is a private residence and is not open to the public.

Birkhall

Birkhall is the Queen Mother's retreat on the Balmoral estate. It is a delightfully secluded small white house, sheltering behind a steep wooded hillside. It has always been used as a summer home for members of the Royal Family. Both the Queen and Princess Margaret enjoyed idyllic childhood days here before the war.

Birkhall is a private residence and is not open to the public.

The Castle of Mey

Shortly after the death of her husband, George VI, in 1952, the Queen Mother went to stay with close friends Lady Doris and Commander Vyner at Dunnet Head in the far north of Scotland. One afternoon, they visited ancient and neglected Barrogill Castle at Thurso, which was up for sale but in an advanced state of disrepair. The roof had been badly damaged by storms, and the interior was damp and decaying. The Queen Mother fell in love with the place. She came back to see it twice that June and five times in August before deciding to buy it. She then gave it back its original name, the Castle of Mey.

The Queen Mother took an active role in the three-year renovation program, buying much of the furniture from local antique shops. The gardens especially were her pride and joy, and she took great care laying them out. The task was complete by 1955—not that a garden is ever finished. The Queen and Prince Philip, invited to a housewarming party, arrived in style on board the royal yacht *Britannia*.

Mey is not a large castle, but it is one of a very few sixteenth-century houses left in the area, with tall, battlemented towers that give it a very romantic feel. Inside, a double staircase leads to the formal dining room and the drawing room, both with stirring views out to sea. A spiral staircase leads up again to Her Majesty's writing room and her bedroom, with paneled walls painted in aquamarine.

The Castle of Mey is a private residence and is not open to the public.

Clarence House

Clarence House is the London home of Queen Elizabeth the Queen Mother. Although physically attached to St. James's Palace, it is in all other ways quite separate.

It began life as an outbuilding to St. James's Palace until, at the end of the eighteenth century, it became the London home of the Duke of Clarence, third son of George III. The Duke, very unlike his elder brother the Prince Regent, later George IV, was perfectly happy with his modest house. All the same, following his marriage to Princess Adelaide, he called in John Nash to give the place a face-lift. In 1830 the Duke succeeded his brother, becoming William IV ("Sailor Bill"), and Clarence House reverted to its role as a lesser royal residence. So it remained until, in 1947, it became the first family home of Princess Elizabeth and Prince Philip.

The Queen Mother has lived here since the death of George VI in 1952. With her customary good taste, she has redecorated the interior, restoring much of the original Georgian elegance. Her Majesty is a noted connoisseur and has large collections of Chelsea and Worcester porcelain, together with a wide range of pictures by artists such as Stubbs, Monet, Sickert, Augustus John, and even Sir Noel Coward, who was a firm friend.

Clarence House is a private residence and is not open to the public; however, it is the scene every year of a charmingly informal royal event. On August 4, the Queen Mother's birthday, she and her family step outside the house to wave to the assembled well-wishers. It's a delightful moment, and affords a wonderful, if brief, close-up view of the family at its most natural and unaffected. For full details, see "August" in *The Royal Year*.

- **Address:** Clarence House, Clarence Row, London SW1.
- **Getting There:** *Tube*—Green Park.

Gatcombe Park

The Gatcombe estate at Minchinhampton in Gloucestershire was bought by the Queen in 1976 for Princess Anne and Captain Mark Phillips. She paid its previous owner, Lord Butler of Saffron Walden, half a million pounds for the house and its 750 acres. Before moving into Gatcombe Park, Princess Anne and her husband had lived in Army accommodations, though the Princess also prudently retained a suite of rooms at Buckingham Palace. When Captain Phillips resigned his commission, he and his wife needed to find both a home *and* a new career for him, preferably in farming. Gatcombe Park's acreage of prime farming land, boosted by an additional 500 acres or so, rented from one of the Queen's neighboring properties, proved the ideal solution. The estate is run as a commercial farm, and is also the site of a series of two-day horse trials.

The house itself, no more than eight miles from the Prince and Princess of Wales's country home, Highgrove, was built about 1770. It is a charming Georgian country house, hung with jasmine and wisteria. On each side of the pedimented central block are pretty bowed wings, while to the west of the building is the original conservatory.

The interior of the building was redecorated for the Princess and her husband by David Hicks, who made it comfortable and intimate while retaining many of the grander features, notably the sturdy Doric columns in the hall and the handsome marble chimneypieces in the principal rooms.

Much work has also gone into modernizing the stables—only natural given the "horsy" background of their owners. Even a heated footbath for the horses has been installed.

Gatcombe Park is a private residence and is not open to the public. However, the grounds are open in August for horse trials. For full details, see "August" in *The Royal Year*.

Highgrove

Highgrove, near Tetbury in Gloucestershire, is the Cotswolds country home of the Prince and Princess of Wales, lying in one of the most beautiful parts of England. The house and 350-acre estate were bought by the Prince for around one million pounds

Highgrove

from the family of Harold Macmillan, the former Conservative Prime Minister.

The house dates from the late eighteenth century. It is a fine neo-classical building, typical of its period, constructed of pale gold Cotswold stone. There are nine main bedrooms, six bathrooms, and a heated swimming pool. The four principal rooms include a fine drawing room with a marble fireplace, and a large library. But there is said to be one feature not normally found in the English country house: an impregnable steel-lined room, for use in the event of a terrorist attack.

South African–born designer Dudley Poplak, who was responsible for the decoration of the couple's suite at Kensington Palace, was charged with decorating Highgrove. He worked closely with the Prince and Princess, aiming at a light, airy effect, with the emphasis on comfort rather than grandeur.

For Prince Charles, one of the great pleasures of Highgrove is its gardens. He has worked long and hard to create the marvelously natural and in many ways original layout, and is especially proud of the large walled garden.

Highgrove is a private residence and is not open to the public.

Nether Lypiatt Manor

Prince and Princess Michael of Kent bought this delightful country house near Stroud in Gloucestershire shortly after their marriage in 1978. An architectural historian working for the National Trust once described it as "this wonderful little house, the ideal country house."

It was built about 1705. Although small, it boasts a rich wooden staircase, and a lovely hall chimneypiece of white stone against blue slate. Princess Michael, a professional interior decorator, oversaw all the restoration and design herself. She has produced a home of great style and elegance.

Nether Lypiatt Manor is a private residence and is not open to the public.

Sandringham

Sandringham House

If the Queen were ever to retire, Sandringham is the place she would come to. Her 20,000-acre estate near King's Lynn in Norfolk provides the thing she enjoys most: a place to breed thoroughbred horses and gun dogs. Every New Year the Queen and her family vacation here, where the lonely cry of the curlew is the only sound that breaks the silence of the bleak landscape.

Their very isolation is what the royals love most about these rolling acres. Picnics on the beach, tramps across the muddy bracken, pheasant shooting, horse riding, the chance to escape the glare of publicity for a few precious days—Sandringham brings out all that is most English in the Royal Family.

From the outside, Sandringham House looms like a large girls' boarding school. Yet it is the most intimate of the Queen's residences. Its mock Jacobean exterior encloses 270 rooms, but the royal home is essentially a mixture of the simple and the grand. It is a regal retreat where valuable Goya portraits hang above clotheshorses bedecked with Christmas cards, where the Queen will feed her corgis breadsticks under the table at a formal black-tie dinner. "It has a smell of polish and freshly picked flowers," recalls one guest. "It is comfortable and very welcoming."

Locals are used to the sight of the Queen in green mackintosh and rubber boots driving the narrow country lanes at the wheel of a battered Land Rover. She goes to the parish church on Sundays, and is a member of the local Women's Institute, where she gives a talk every year and judges the jam-making and flower-arranging competitions.

The estate was bought by Queen Victoria for her son the Prince of Wales, later Edward VII, in the hope that it would keep her errant boy away from dissolute London life. The Prince, however, merely imported his smart friends to Sandringham, where he threw vast parties with gargantuan meals, the air thick with cigar smoke and racy talk. Later, the floorboards creaked as guests stole down the corridors in pursuit of further diversions. It was all very different from the dusty grandeur of Victoria's court. (Edward's motto was that you could do anything so long as you didn't frighten the horses.) The Prince introduced other sporting pleasures in the shape of pheasant shooting, a tradition maintained with equal success today by Prince Philip. In 1891 Sandringham was rebuilt and enlarged following a serious fire. The present Queen, however, has had 91 rooms demolished, feeling that the house had simply grown too large.

When the Queen is in residence she enjoys showing visitors her stud farms at Wolferton and Sandringham. An acknowledged bloodstock expert, Her Majesty usually visits the studs three times a week. She makes sure she always has a pocketful of mints to feed her horses. At her kennels, where she breeds sleek black Labrador gun dogs, the Queen is happy to fetch and carry food and water in metal buckets.

The estate grows blackcurrants, strawberries, sugar beets, peas, and beans. Fall visitors in their thousands spend many happy hours in the orchards picking their own fruit.

Besides the gardens, with their early summer displays of azaleas and rhododendrons, the estate contains a country park and a museum of estate memorabilia, as well as exhibitions of gifts received by the Queen on overseas tours and of vintage royal cars.

- **Address:** Sandringham House, King's Lynn, Norfolk (tel. 0553–772675).

- **Getting There:** *By Car*—From London take the M11 to exit 14 and then the A10 to King's Lynn. From there, take the A148 to Fakenham and then the B1440 to Sandringham.

- **House and Grounds:** Open April 19 through Sept. 24, Mon. to Thurs., 11–4:45 (grounds 10:30–5), Sun. 12–4:45 (grounds 11:30–5), closed. Fri. and Sat. House also closed July 20 through Aug. 8, and grounds closed July 24 through Aug. 5. These times may change, so call for latest information and admission charges.

Thatched House Lodge

This early-eighteenth-century brick-built house is the home of Her Royal Highness Princess Alexandra and her husband, the Honorable Angus Ogilvy. It stands in Richmond Park, on the southwestern outskirts of London. Despite its closeness to the capital, the house seems almost to be lost in the country.

Thatched House Lodge was originally built around 1673 as a hunting lodge. In 1725 George II bought it and gave it to one of the Park Rangers, who was son of the then Prime Minister, Sir Robert Walpole. In 1727 the house was rebuilt, becoming the handsome edifice it is today.

The Princess and her husband bought the house in 1963,

shortly after their wedding, and both their children were born here—James in 1964 and Marina in 1966.

Thatched House Lodge is a private residence and is not open to the public.

ROYAL CONNECTIONS———————

Althrop

Althrop, pronounced "Alltrup," is the family home of the Princess of Wales, the former Lady Diana Spencer. Located a few miles north of Northampton, about seventy miles from London, it has been the ancestral seat of the Spencers since 1508, when the original house was built by Sir John Spencer. Today it is lived in by Princess Diana's father, the amiably eccentric Earl Spencer, and his wife, Countess Raine Spencer, daughter of best-selling romantic novelist and sage Barbara Cartland.

The house, largely rebuilt in 1790 and substantially renovated in 1982, is filled with the Spencers' sumptuous family treasures: superb furniture, china, and pictures, including many magnificent family portraits. However, visitors hoping for exhibits on Princess Diana will be disappointed.

But Diana's absence is amply compensated by the presence of Earl Spencer. Unlike many of England's stately home owners, he is frequently spotted greeting visitors and helping in the souvenir shop. He has even been seen watching television by visitors wandering through his drawing room, proof indeed that despite its grandeur Althrop remains very much a family home.

- *Address:* Althrop, Northampton, Northamptonshire (tel. 0604–770209).

- *House and Grounds:* Open daily 1:30–5:30; June, July, Aug., and bank holidays 11–6. Admission £2.50, children £1.25; gardens 50p; Wed., Connoisseurs' Day (longer tour), £3.50.

- *Getting There: By Car*—From London take M1 expressway to exit 16 and follow signs on A428 to Althrop.

Broadlands

Located just a few miles north of Southampton in the pretty Hampshire countryside, Broadlands owes its links with the Royal Family to Lord Mountbatten, grandson of Queen Victoria, uncle of Prince Philip, and long Prince Charles's confidant and mentor.

Daring, ambitious, and charming, in 1923 Mountbatten married Lady Edwina Ashley. She was an unusual woman, headstrong and unreliable, but immensely wealthy. Through her, he inherited Broadlands, an imposing eighteenth-century mansion designed by Capability Brown, the eighteenth-century's most famous landscape gardener, who also laid out the sweeping park. In the nineteenth century the house was owned by that fearsome prime minister, Lord Palmerston.

Its interior is grandly sumptuous. A series of portraits by Van Dyck, Reynolds, and Lawrence compete for attention with a striking collection of Wedgwood and a fine assembly of ancient sculptures.

In recent times the house has seen many royal visits. In 1947 Princess Elizabeth and Prince Philip spent much of their honeymoon here. And in 1981 Prince Charles and his bride spent the first night of their honeymoon here before flying off to Gibraltar and the royal yacht *Britannia*. In his bachelor days the Prince also passed many weekends at Broadlands, especially when his minesweeper, H.M.S. *Bronington,* was berthed at nearby Portsmouth. The sympathetic and discreet atmosphere engendered by Mountbatten at Broadlands is said to have provided an ideal environment for the Prince's many dalliances.

When Mountbatten opened his house to the public in 1979, it was Prince Charles who performed the ceremony. Mountbatten was assassinated by the I.R.A. just a few months later. Fittingly, when in May 1981 a special exhibition on the life and times of Lord Mountbatten was mounted at Broadlands, it was Charles, accompanied by his fiancee, who opened it.

- *Address:* Broadlands, Romsey, Hampshire (tel. 0794–516878).

- *Getting There: By Car*—Eight miles north of Southampton on the A3057, entrance from A31 immediately south of Romsey. From London take the M3, then M27; take exit 3 to the A31.

- *House and Grounds:* Open April through Sept., Tues. to Sun., 10–6, closed. Mon. except in Aug., Sept., and bank holidays. Admission £ 3, children 12 to 16 £1.70, senior citizens £2.20, children under 12 free.

Glamis Castle

Glamis Castle

Glamis Castle, pronounced "Glarms," a few miles north of Dundee in Scotland's Tayside, has been the seat of the Bowes-Lyon family, the Queen Mother's family, for more than 600 years. It is also the legendary setting of much of Shakespeare's *Macbeth*. Today it is owned by the seventeenth Earl of Strathmore and Kinghorne, the Queen Mother's nephew.

The Queen Mother has many fond memories of this childhood home. As a youngster she kept a pet pig here. As a young woman she tended the wounded from the trenches of World War I. In 1923, as Duchess of York, she spent her honeymoon at Glamis. And Princess Margaret was born here, in 1930, the first immediate member of the Royal Family born in Scotland since 1602. Her Majesty frequently returns to savor the peace and quiet of this sturdy Scottish retreat.

But the castle has a darker side, too. It is reputed to be haunted by a number of ghosts. Until well into this century there was also reputed to be a huge and hideous ape-like creature at large in the castle—the Monster of Glamis. He is said to have lived for 140 years, imprisoned within the gloomy gray walls of the castle, allowed out only at nights, when he would prowl along the roofs.

- *Address:* Glamis Castle, Glamis, Tayside, Scotland (tel. 030784—242).

- *House and Grounds:* Open Easter and May through Sept., Sun. to Fri. 1–5; closed Sat. Admission £2.

- *Getting There: By Car*—12 miles north of Dundee on A928.

Osborne House

Osborne House, located near Cowes on the Isle of Wight just off the south coast of England, was the seaside home of Queen Victoria and Prince Albert. But thoughts of some small rose-clad cottage nestling in the lee of protective hills are misleading. For Osborne is decidedly large, even palatial, despite attempts by Victoria and her husband to instill in it a degree of domesticity.

The original house here was bought by Victoria and Albert in 1845. As at Balmoral, the Queen and her consort had it demolished almost immediately, putting up in its place today's elegantly sturdy Italianate mansion. Though designed by Thomas Cubitt, a fashionable architect of the day, it bears the stamp of Prince Albert's busy and inquisitive mind, right down to the central heating that the much-maligned Prince Consort had installed.

It is a graceful house, still very much as it was when Victoria died here in January 1901, with handsome rose-filled formal gardens leading to spacious lawns bordered by bulging shrubberies and tall trees. There is much that calls to mind a prim Victorian summer afternoon, with sweeping skirts, frock coats, croquet on the lawn, the muted clink of silver spoons on china, and wafer-thin bread and butter.

For all the grandeur of the house and its setting, the Queen and Albert tried hard to make Osborne as ordinary a family home as they could. But even the Swiss Cottage, a sort of gigantic doll's house which they built in the gardens for their nine children, has a grim, Teutonic quality to it. Edward VII certainly had few happy memories of the place. He lost no time donating Osborne to the nation after his mother died. And here it still is, full of Victorian bric-a-brac, a somehow melancholy memorial to the great Queen Empress.

- **Address:** Osborne House, East Cowes, Isle of Wight (tel. 0983–200022).

- **House and Grounds:** Open April to mid-Oct., Mon. to Sat., 10–5, Sun. 11–5. Admission £2.20, senior citizens £1.65, under 16s £1.10.

- **Getting There:** Ferry or hydrofoil from Southampton to Cowes. The house is one mile southeast of Cowes on the East Cowes Road.

The Royal Yacht *Britannia*

The Queen's floating palace, the royal yacht *Britannia,* is the oldest ship in the Royal Navy and the best loved. Since she was launched in 1952 she has traveled more than 720,000 miles and visited 580 ports, in the process circumnavigating the world seven times.

Over the years the members of the Royal Family have come to cherish her. She is as much a part of them as Balmoral and Sandringham, and on board her they have learned to paint and photograph, have honeymooned and holidayed, have played the fool on deck, and sung sea shanties around the black baby grand piano. Endless banquets and receptions have been given in her lavish state rooms.

Britannia holds a special place in the Queen's heart, for in Prince Philip's words, "She is special for a number of reasons. Almost every previous sovereign has been responsible for a building, a church, a castle, a palace, or just a house. William the Conqueror built the Tower of London, Edward I built the Welsh castles, Edward IV built St. George's Chapel at Windsor, and Edward VII built Sandringham. The only comparable structure built in the present reign is *Britannia.* As such she is a splendid example of contemporary British design and technology and much admired wherever she is seen, particularly on official visits overseas."

She carries a crew of 276, including a 26-piece Royal Marine band, and can even find space for a gleaming Rolls-Royce if required. The 412-foot yacht is used by the Royal Family during Cowes week, when it is moored in Portsmouth harbor; for its annual cruise of the Western Isles of Scotland; and for overseas visits including, in the recent past, California and New York. Wherever she goes she is a wonderful emblem of both seamanship and all that is best in British naval traditions.

Besides being used by the Royal Family she also acts as a

floating conference center where British businessmen invite their foreign counterparts to sample their goods and services.

She has been used as a honeymoon hotel for several royal couples—Princess Margaret and Anthony Armstrong-Jones, Prince Charles and Princess Diana, and the Duke and Duchess of York. The sight of her entering or leaving port has created a lasting impression around the world. As former royal courtier Sir Rupert Neville says: "The dramatic effect of the royal yacht leaving port with thousands of cheering people watching the Queen go is enormous."

ROYAL SHOPPING

Shopping for the Royal Family would seem to be a great pleasure, given not only the depth of the royal purse but the fact that any shop with even the merest hint of royal patronage will go to almost any lengths to attract its prospective royal customers.

But the reality is rather different. While minor royals can, and do, head out to the shops much as any mere mortal might, for the majority of the Royal Family the ever-present security risks, coupled with the problems of dealing with onlookers, prying journalists, and photographers, make public shopping an ordeal to be avoided. These drawbacks, however, do not deter the younger royals, especially those who married into the Royal Family—Princess Diana, for example, or the Duchess of York— who enjoyed ordinary lives before their dramatic elevation to royal superstardom. These royals can still be seen around the smart London shops, particularly in Knightsbridge, in the area bounded by Harrods, Beauchamp (pronounced "Beecham") Place, and the Harvey Nichols department store.

The Royal Warrant

Four members of the Royal Family—the Queen, Prince Philip, the Prince of Wales, and the Queen Mother—have it within their gift to bestow on a select number of shops the royal warrant, a sort of regal stamp of approval and a public announcement that a particular shop is where the Queen buys her hats, or where Prince Philip gets his hair cut. It's a fiercely sought-after honor, with the chosen shops—and there are less than 900 of them—able to display the coat of arms of their royal patron. Although a shop may hold warrants from more than one member of the Royal Family, no more than a handful hold them from all four.

Naturally enough, the bulk of the royal warrant holders are in London. But the little Scottish town of Ballater, in all other respects a pretty humdrum sort of place, boasts a disproportionately large number of royal warrants. The reason, simply, is that the Queen's Scottish holiday home, Balmoral, is nearby. The Scottish capital, Edinburgh, is also home to a significant number of royal warrant holders.

To become eligible for the honor, a shop or business must have supplied goods or services to the Royal Family for at least three consecutive years. Once granted, the warrant will be reviewed every ten years. But it can be canceled at any time, and—the royal will being tantamount to a command—no reason need be given.

Our listings here contain only a sampling of the most celebrated royal shops. For the dedicated royalty watcher—and gourmand—we have also included a small number of especially favored royal restaurants.

ROYAL STYLE—HERS

Aquascutum
100 Regent Street
London W1A 2AO
(01–734 6090)
Makers of weatherproof garments to HM The Queen Mother.
The name is Latin for "water protection," and you'll find no lack of it at this smart shop selling classic English raincoats and separates. The quality clothes are at the very top of the fashion pyramid—as are the prices.

Asprey & Company
165–169 New Bond Street
London W1Y OAR
(01–493 6767)
Goldsmiths, silversmiths, and jewelers to HM The Queen and HRH The Prince of Wales, and jewelers to HM The Queen Mother.
Located on one of London's best-known streets for chic shopping, Aspreys has been described as the "classiest and most luxurious shop in the world." It offers a range of exquisite jewelry and gifts, both antique and modern. If you're in the market for a six-branched Georgian candelabrum or a six-carat emerald and diamond brooch, you won't be disappointed.

Bellville Sassoon
73 Pavillion Road
London SW1X OET
(01–235 3087)
A favorite of the always fashionable Princess of Wales; David Sassoon designed her honeymoon outfit as well as the pink *crepe de Chine* dress she wore for Prince William's christening. His ballgowns, in particular, are famous in London society.

Benetton

23 Brompton Road
London SW3 1ED (and branches)
(01–589 6503)
Benetton's bright and trendy casual clothing for men, women, and children are ever popular. Highly favored by the Princess of Wales, this Italian company's designs are inexpensive and fun to wear.

Benny Ong

3 Bentinck Mews
London W1M 5FL
(01–487 5954)
Originally from Singapore, Benny Ong came to England to study fashion in the heady '60s. Today his designs are worn by everyone, from the Princess of Wales to the Prime Minister of Iceland.

Bradley's

83 Knightsbridge
London SW1X 7RB
(01–235 2902)
Without doubt, this is the largest specialist lingerie store in all England, with styles ranging from warm and sensible undies and nightgowns to the most glamorous silk and satin lace camisoles and French knickers. Customers include the Princess of Wales, Princess Anne, and many European and Saudi royal families.

Bruce Oldfield

27 Beauchamp Place
London SW3 1NX
(01–584 1363)
Bruce Oldfield has been called the "golden boy" of British fashion, a reputation in large measure due to his enduring popularity with the Princess of Wales. She has been wearing both his day and evening wear ever since her engagement, while a good number of the outfits for her tours of Canada and Australia have been Oldfield designs. His trade mark is a sensuously feminine style, a style that has won over such lesser mortals as Joan Collins.

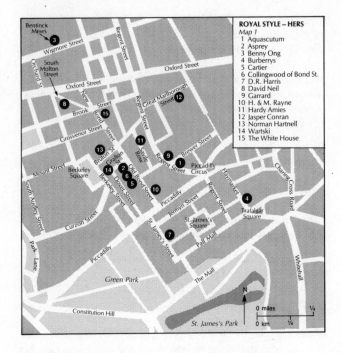

ROYAL STYLE – HERS
Map 1
1 Aquascutum
2 Asprey
3 Benny Ong
4 Burberrys
5 Cartier
6 Collingwood of Bond St.
7 D.R. Harris
8 David Neil
9 Garrard
10 H. & M. Rayne
11 Hardy Amies
12 Jasper Conran
13 Norman Hartnell
14 Wartski
15 The White House

Burberry's

18 The Haymarket
London SW1Y 4DQ
(01–930 3343)
Weatherproofers to HM The Queen and HM The Queen Mother.
A name synonymous with English style. The Burberry raincoat is a classic, known the world over. The unmistakable Burberry plaid also adorns an array of umbrellas, scarves, handbags, hats, and belts.

Calman Links

241 Brompton Road
London SW3 1LX
(01–581 1927)
Furriers to HM The Queen and HM The Queen Mother.
This posh Knightsbridge shop deals in both ready-to-wear and made-to-measure furs, all of the highest quality. Cleaning and

152

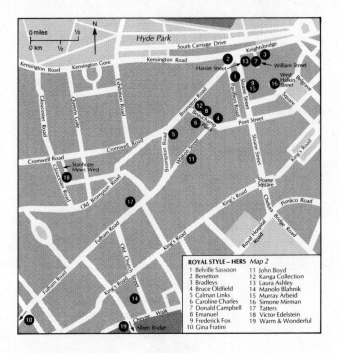

ROYAL STYLE – HERS *Map 2*

1 Belville Sassoon	11 John Boyd
2 Benetton	12 Kanga Collection
3 Bradleys	13 Laura Ashley
4 Bruce Oldfield	14 Manolo Blahnik
5 Calman Links	15 Murray Arbeid
6 Caroline Charles	16 Simone Mirman
7 Donald Campbell	17 Tatters
8 Emanuel	18 Victor Edelstein
9 Frederick Fox	19 Warm & Wonderful
10 Gina Fratini	

storage is also offered at Calman Links, which claims to look after its customers' furs "from the cradle to the grave."

Caroline Charles

11 Beauchamp Place
London SW3 1NQ
(01–589 5850)
The Princess of Wales began buying ready-to-wear clothing from Caroline Charles before her engagement to Prince Charles, and has continued to do so ever since. Ms. Charles's delightful day and evening wear is inspired by national costumes and old cinema.

Cartier

175 New Bond Street
London W1Y 2JH
(01–493 6962)
Jewelers and goldsmiths to HM The Queen and HM The Queen Mother.

153

With a world-wide reputation as one of the most elegant and discriminating of jewelers, Cartiers was granted its first royal warrant in 1904. It has continued ever since to supply jewelry and gifts to the Royal Family, as well as to the rich and famous. Its New Bond Street showroom is the last word in luxurious good taste. Some of the best-known jewels that appeared in the Geneva sale of the Duchess of Windsor's trinkets first saw the light of day here.

Collingwood of Bond Street
171 New Bond Street
London W1Y 9PB
(01–734 2656)
Jewelers and silversmiths to HM The Queen and jewelers to HM The Queen Mother.
Collingwood has been making wedding bands for the Royal Family for more than 100 years. It wrought those of the Queen Mother, the Queen, Princess Margaret, and the Princess of Wales from the same Welsh gold nugget. More recently, it created the very lovely necklace of cultured pearls and diamonds with a central heart which the Prince of Wales gave to Princess Diana following the birth of their first son, Prince William.

D. R. Harris & Company
29 St. James's Street
London SW1A 1HB
(01–930 8753)
Chemists to HM The Queen Mother.
This family business has served the gentry and Court of St. James's since 1790 ("chemist" is, of course, the British word for pharmacist). It offers a wonderful array of secret concoctions made to order by Mr. Harris, including the ever-popular Milk of Cucumber and Roses and a Pick-Me-Up still as effective a hangover cure today as it was a century ago.

David Neil
38 South Molton Street
London W1Y 1HA
(01–408 1021)
Another designer patronized by the Princess of Wales, David Neil is best known and loved for his marvelous wedding gown confections.

Donald Campbell

8 William Street
London SW1X 9HL
(01–235 3332)

A designer who has made many outfits for the Princess of Wales also has a very popular ready-to-wear collection. His most popular item—a typically English "afternoon" dress in floral silk—strikes exactly the right chord at Buckingham Palace garden parties.

Emanuel

10 Beauchamp Place
London SW3 1NQ
(01–584 4997)

David and Elizabeth Emanuel shot to fame after designing the fairy-tale wedding gown worn by Lady Diana Spencer at her marriage to Prince Charles. Their designs have remained a firm favorite with the Princess for both day and evening wear. The Emanuels' popularity, particularly for wedding and ball gowns, is now immense.

Frederick Fox

169 Sloane Street
London SW1X 9QF
(01–235 5618)

Milliner to HM The Queen.

Frederick Fox has for years been making hats for several members of the Royal Family, including the Queen and Princess Diana. Mr. Fox is also patronized by numerous society women and politicians' and diplomats' wives.

Garrard & Company

112 Regent Street
London W1A 2JJ
(01–734 7020)

Goldsmiths and Crown Jewelers to HM The Queen and HM The Queen Mother.

Garrards were appointed crown jewelers by Queen Victoria in 1843, but its connection with the Royal Family dates back further still, to 1722. Today Garrards is responsible for looking after the Crown Jewels, a process which involves spending two weeks every year in the Tower of London, where the jewels are housed, as well as preparing the jewels and accompanying regalia for coronations and state occasions.

Although Garrards comes into its own when dealing with occasions of state, it still sees itself as a family jeweler, and offers an enormous range of items ranging from the antique to the modern. It will also design and create jewelry to a client's own requirements. Its most famous piece was the engagement ring that Prince Charles gave to Lady Diana Spencer.

Gina Fratini
Marvic House
Bishops Road
London SW6 7AD
(01–381 8759)

Ms. Fratini's formal and sophisticated designs—mainly evening wear—show a great attention to detail. They have captured the royal attention of the Princess of Wales, Princess Anne, Princess Alexandra, and the Duchess of Kent.

H. & M. Rayne
15 Old Bond Street
London W1X 3DB
(01–493 9077)

Shoemakers to HM The Queen and HM The Queen Mother.
This royal shoemaker designs classic, stylish, and, above all, comfortable shoes (the inimitable "sensible" English shoe), as frequently sported by the Queen, the Queen Mother, and Princess Margaret. Raynes is especially good on smart walking shoes, a must when spending most of the day on your feet as the Queen does.

Hardy Amies
14 Savile Row
London W1X 1JN
(01–734 2436)

Dressmakers to HM The Queen.
Hardy Amies has been designing clothes for the Queen since her tour of Canada in 1948. In 1977, as a mark of her high favor, she made him a Commander of the Royal Victorian Order. Mr. Amies' shop is housed in a fine Georgian building in Savile Row, a street name synonymous with impeccably traditional English tailoring. His collections are classics of the highest quality, if occasionally a trifle staid. But their creator sees them very much as a fashion investment.

Jasper Conran

49–50 Great Marlborough Street
London W1V 1DB
(01–437 0386)

Jasper Conran's collections are much sought after by Princess Diana and a string of other high-profile women, including actress Joan Collins and television personality Paula Yates, wife of Bob Geldof. Ms. Yates's unusual red wedding dress was a Conran creation—and he also made a copy in miniature for their daughter, Fifi. Jasper is the son of well-known and successful parents—his mother authored *Superwoman* and *Lace,* among other books; his father is the driving force behind the nationwide chain of Habitat, Heals, Conran's, and Mothercare stores.

Laura Ashley

9 Harriet Street
London SW1X 9JS (and branches)
(01–235 9796)

The very pretty Laura Ashley fabrics and wallpapers create an essentially English look which has become strikingly popular in recent years. The women's and children's clothing is often evocative of past eras, with lashings of laces and soft floral prints. Designs are simple yet effective, with an easy-to-wear styling, and prices are within reach of even a non-royal pocketbook.

John Boyd

91 Walton Street
London SW3 2HP
(01–589 7601)

A firm favorite with many members of the Royal Family, John Boyd has been making hats for Princess Anne since she was a teenager, and for the Princess of Wales since her engagement. He designed the stylish tricorne she wore with her honeymoon outfit. He also makes headwear for the natty Mrs. Thatcher.

Kanga Collection

8 Beauchamp Place
London SW3 1NQ
(01–581 1185)

Lady Dale ("Kanga") Tryon, close friend and confidante of Prince Charles, owns this shop which sells her distinctive day and evening wear. The Princess of Wales is a regular customer, naturally.

Manolo Blahnik

49 Old Church Street
London SW3 5BS
(01–352 3863)

Blahnik's beautifully crafted and elegantly conceived shoes are much loved by the Princess of Wales and the Duchess of York, who had "a drawerful" as part of her wedding trousseau. Widely recognized as one of the world's top shoe designers, Mr. Blahnik sells his footwear at prices upwards of £150.

Murray Arbeid

169 Sloane Street
London SW1X 9QP
(01–235 5618)

Specializing mainly in cocktail and evening dresses, Mr. Arbeid considers his sophisticated designs more successful in the United States than in England because of what he calls the glittering *Dallas* quality of American social life. The Princess of Wales, however, is one Englishwoman who finds his clothing designs much to her taste, and is a frequent client.

Norman Hartnell

26 Bruton Street
London W1X 8DD
(01–629 0992)

Dressmakers to HM The Queen and HM The Queen Mother.
Sir Norman Hartnell began designing for the Royal Family in 1935, when he created a wedding dress for Lady Alice Montagu-Douglas-Scott on her marriage to the Duke of Gloucester; two of the bridesmaids were the young Princesses Elizabeth and Margaret. The following year he began designing for the Duchess of York, now the Queen Mother. Mr. Hartnell remained one of the Queen Mother's most favored designers until his death in 1979. The House of Hartnell, however, still continues to serve the Royal Family from its splendid, luxurious showrooms in Mayfair's Bruton Street.

Simone Mirman

11 West Halkin Street
London SW1X 8JL
(01–235 2656)

Milliner to HM The Queen and HM The Queen Mother.
The milliner who thinks that "your hat should make you feel like singing" has for many years created fashion arias for the Queen,

the Queen Mother, and Princess Margaret, as well as for many
non-royal notables including the late Vivien Leigh, Bianca Jagger, and Elizabeth Taylor.

Tatters
74 Fulham Road
London SW3 5PF
(01–584 1532)
Held in high esteem for its collection of romantic and berib-
boned ballgowns and wedding dresses, Tatters is another shop
frequented by the Princess of Wales. She ordered much of her
stylish maternity clothing from here.

Victor Edelstein
9 Stanhope Mews West
London SW3 5RB
(01–373 5462)
Another designer who has won the Princess of Wales's favor,
Mr. Edelstein sells only made-to-order clothing, and sees his
well-heeled customers by appointment only. His designs are
characterized by formal, classic, and very sophisticated lines.

Warm & Wonderful
919 St. John's Hill
London SW11 1TH
(01–228 8724)
Specializing in hand- and machine-knitted woolen sweaters,
this charming shop was catapulted to fame by the Princess of
Wales, who was photographed in one of its "black-sheep"
creations—a red background covered in rows of white sheep
with a single black one nosing his way in. Good for casual and
fun designs, as well as more sleek styles.

Wartski
14 Grafton Street
London W1X 3LA
(01–493 1141)
*Jewelers to HM The Queen, HM The Queen Mother, and HRH
The Prince of Wales.*
Since 1925, Wartski has been renowned for its fabulous collection of Faberge jewelry and objets d'art. Its first royal warrant
was granted by Queen Mary, who collected Faberge; the interest has since been maintained by both the Queen and the
Queen Mother.

The White House

51–52 New Bond Street
London W1Y 0BY
(01–629 3521)

The White House says its children's clothes are "for everybody's little prince and princess" (though only if Mommy and Daddy have a pocketful of cash to spend). Certainly the Princess of Wales browses a great deal here for the Princes William and Harry. She bought their classic silk romper suits, handsmocked and embroidered, here; they were worn by both princes as babies and toddlers. Besides its delightful children's wear, the White House also has an extensive array of handmade lingerie and table linens.

ROYAL STYLE—HIS _____

Ashley & Blake

42 Beauchamp Place
London SW3 1NX
(01–584 2682)
Shirtmakers to HRH The Duke of Edinburgh.
A charmingly traditional shop selling classic cotton shirts, suits, and lovely cashmere and wool sweaters for men and women. Elegance, style, and tradition rule supreme here.

Floris

89 Jermyn Street
London SW1Y 6JH
(01–930 2885)
Perfumers to HM The Queen and manufacturers of toilet preparations to HRH The Prince of Wales.
Floris's exquisite interior gleams with satin-lined mahogany showcases, originally built for the Great Exhibition of 1851 in the Crystal Palace. The 18 exclusive fragrances that Floris creates have been produced by the family for over five generations, and feature in a wide range of toiletries made from sandalwood, lily of the valley, tuberose, and other subtle aromas. A delightful shop offering a real taste of timeless English style.

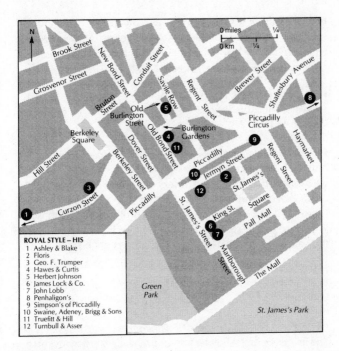

ROYAL STYLE – HIS
1 Ashley & Blake
2 Floris
3 Geo. F. Trumper
4 Hawes & Curtis
5 Herbert Johnson
6 James Lock & Co.
7 John Lobb
8 Penhaligon's
9 Simpson's of Piccadilly
10 Swaine, Adeney, Brigg & Sons
11 Truefitt & Hill
12 Turnbull & Asser

Geo. F. Trumper

9 Curzon Street
London W1Y 7FL
(01–499 1850)
Hairdresser to HM The Queen.
Although the legend outside the shop reads "Court Hairdresser and Perfumer to the late King George V from 1919–1936," its first royal warrant dates back even further, to the reign of Queen Victoria. Today Trumper still blends by hand the same toiletries used by the sovereign 100 years ago.

Hawes & Curtis

2 Burlington Gardens
London W1X 1LH
(01–734 1020)
Tailors to HRH The Duke of Edinburgh.
The Duke of Edinburgh, Prince Charles, the Duke of York, Prince Edward, even Frank Sinatra, shop at this smartly traditional men's outfitters. The late Lord Mountbatten was also a

161

regular customer. Clothes are mostly made to order, though Hawes & Curtis does provide a selection of ready-to-wear suits and shirts. There's also a vast assortment of ties, plus the best offering of bathrobes in London.

Herbert Johnson

13 Old Burlington Street
London W1X 1LA
(01–437 7397)
Hatters to HM The Queen and HRH The Prince of Wales.
Although its specialty lies in sporting and country hats, this well-established firm makes every conceivable type of head-gear, including military hats. The Royal Navy cap worn by Prince Charles for his wedding was from Herbert Johnson. Prices are on the steep side, but a Herbert Johnson hat enjoys the sort of cachet that deserves an inflated price tag.

James Lock & Company

6 St. James's Street
London SW1A 1EF
(01–930 8874)
Hatters to HRH The Duke of Edinburgh.
The inventors of the bowler hat supply headgear to many members of the Royal Family; Prince Charles's polo hats and Princess Diana's riding hats are from here. Other clients include Larry Hagman, better known as *Dallas*'s J. R. Ewing.

John Lobb

9 St. James's Street
London SW1A 1EF
(01–930 3664)
Bootmakers to HM The Queen, HRH The Duke of Edinburgh, and HRH The Prince of Wales.
One of the great English shops, Lobbs has been making beautiful shoes for hundreds of years, and its traditions of craftsmanship and style are still every bit as strong today as they were in the last century. Anyone in search of impeccably made, long-lasting English shoes need look no further.

Penhaligon's

41 Wellington Street
London WC2E 7BN (and branches)
(01–836 2150)

*Manufacturers of toilet requisites to HRH The Duke of Edin-
burgh.*

William Penhaligon—court barber at the end of Queen Victoria's lengthy reign—blended perfumes and toilet waters in the
back of his shop, using essential oils and natural, indeed often
exotic, ingredients. Some of the resulting toiletries were reserved exclusively for important clients, including Lord Roth-
schild and Sir Winston Churchill. Today Penhaligon's still makes
its traditional preparations—including soaps, talc, and bath oils
—following William Penhaligon's original notes, while the elegantly packaged products and equally sumptuous shop both
retain a look of high Victoriana.

Simpsons of Piccadilly

203 Piccadilly
London W1A 2AS
(01–734 2002)
*Outfitters to HM The Queen, HRH The Duke of Edinburgh, and
HRH The Prince of Wales.*

Established in 1894 by Simeon Simpson, this outfitter moved to
its present site—close by Piccadilly Circus—in 1935. Simpsons
sells essentially casual English clothes, with its own label sold
under the name DAKS. Today, the founder's granddaughter,
designer Georgina Simpson, has revamped the store to include
top British, European, and American designers. Her husband,
actor Anthony Andrews (who is probably best known for his
portrayal of the teddybear-cuddling Sebastian Flyte in *Brides-
head Revisited*), wears Simpsons clothes almost exclusively.

Swaine, Adeney, Brigg & Sons

185 Piccadilly
London W1V 0HA
(01–734 4277)
*Whip and glove maker to HM The Queen, umbrella makers to
HM The Queen Mother.*

Swaine, Adeney, Brigg & Sons' location in Piccadilly dates back
to 1750, and the company has been honored with a royal
warrant ever since the reign of George III. You'll find everything
equestrian in this dignified shop, plus hunting and fishing equipment. There's also a fine selection of umbrellas and gloves for
the city slicker.

163

Truefitt & Hill

23 Old Bond Street
London W1X 3DA
(01–493 2961)
Hairdressers to HRH The Duke of Edinburgh.
This wonderfully traditional barber shop will make you feel as
if you've stumbled onto an old film set, but the precision hair-
cuts will convince you otherwise. The most famous customer
has his hair cut in the privacy of Buckingham Palace.

Turnbull & Asser

71–72 Jermyn Street
London SW1Y 6PF
(01–930 0502)
Shirt manufacturers to HRH The Prince of Wales.
Prince Charles buys nearly all his shirts here, though, unlike
most of us, he doesn't need to wait for the yearly sales to do
so. The tailored shirts come in a myriad of patterns. Among the
tasteful accessories are butter-soft, cashmere-lined gloves,
bright silk bow ties, and calfskin suspenders. The bathrobes are
luxurious.

ROYAL LIVING

David Linley Furniture

1 New Kings Road
London SW6 4SB
(01–736 6886)
Princess Margaret's son, David Linley, and his partner Matthew
Rice, opened their shop in October 1985 and have been hard
at work ever since, creating hand-crafted items of furniture
mainly on commission. Their major pieces range from £500 to
several thousand pounds. But a range of desktop accessories,
such as Venetian-style letter holders and notepads, has been
very popular, with price tags a much more affordable £8–£22.

Dragons of Walton Street

23 Walton Street
London SW3 2HX
(01–589 3795)
Expertly crafted and hand-painted wooden nursery furniture
designed by Rosie Fisher is sold here, from wardrobes and toy

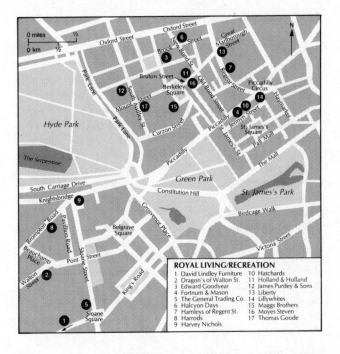

chests to rocking horses and doll houses. Dragons can supply any style and piece of furniture a client wishes, with results that are sure to delight. The Princess of Wales completely decorated her children's nursery at their Highgrove home with Dragons furniture.

Edward Goodyear

45 Brook Street
London W1A 2JQ
(01–629 1508)
Florists to HM The Queen, HM The Queen Mother, HRH The Duke of Edinburgh, and HRH The Prince of Wales.
One of only a handful of shops to hold royal warrants from all four members of the Royal Family entitled to grant them, Edward Goodyear supplies plants and flowers for all occasions, from simple bouquets of daisies to the most elaborate floral arrangements.

Fortnum & Mason
181 Piccadilly
London W1A 1ER
(01–734 8040)
*Grocers and provision merchants to HM The Queen, and sup-
pliers of leather and fancy goods to HM The Queen Mother.*
Famous for its remarkable food hampers—which can be spotted just about anywhere the wealthy gather to picnic—this must
be the ultimate grocery shop. Arranged along its beautifully
displayed shelves is a delicious and extensive selection of teas,
cakes, caviar, *foie gras,* and truffles; in short, just about anything
you might ever want to subsist on, from a simple breakfast to
a bacchanalian feast. There is even a splendid red-liveried gentleman to direct the dazed visitor.

But while Fortnum's is best known for its sumptuous food
hall, the store also has three further floors which sell a high-
quality selection of fashion (men's, women's, and children's),
toys, china, and gifts. There are no less than two tea shops on
the premises, and you might even see a crowd gathering outside
the shop to see the unique clock strike the hour—the cue for
the Messrs. Fortnum and Mason to come out and bow to each
other's enormous success.

The General Trading Company
144 Sloane Street
Sloane Square
London SW1X 9BL
(01–730 0411)
*Suppliers of fancy goods to HM The Queen, HM The Queen
Mother, and HRH The Duke of Edinburgh.*
Rumor has it that the Prince and Princess of Wales had their
wedding gift list at this Sloane Street establishment. With a
dozen departments to peruse, even the most finicky shopper
will find something to delight or amuse him or her in this Alad-
din's cave of treasures. The General Trading Company buyers
continually travel the world to discover new suppliers, and
merchandise covers the range from classic English china to
French glass, from Indian crafts to Italian lighting. This is one of
those delightfully diverting shops where you can spend as little
as £5 or as much as your credit card will stretch to—and always
feel you are walking away with something special.

Halcyon Days

14 Brook Street
London W1Y 1AA
(01–629 8811)
Suppliers of objets d'art to HM The Queen and HM The Queen Mother.
This is a charming shop devoted entirely to decorative boxes of every type, material, and size, from music to snuff boxes, made of china, enamel, or precious metals. Halcyon Days promise its boxes will be the antiques of tomorrow. Princess Diana, at least, seems satisfied with the truth of this claim.

Hamleys of Regent Street

188–196 Regent Street
London W1R 5DF
(01–734 3161)
Toy and sports merchants to HM The Queen.
The world's biggest toy shop, and one of the very best, Hamleys was given its first royal warrant in 1938 by Queen Mary. There are acres of toys here, from porcelain dolls to computer games. The sheer selection can be overwhelming, especially on a crowded day. Some traditionalists feel the store has rather too exuberantly embraced the world of videos and Space Invaders, but the doll houses and pedal cars, rocking horses and Steiff animals are as winning as ever.

Harrods

Knightsbridge
London SW1X 7XL
(01–730 1234)
Suppliers of provisions and household goods to HM The Queen, suppliers of china, glass, and fancy goods to HM The Queen Mother, and outfitters to HRH The Duke of Edinburgh and HRH The Prince of Wales.
One of the world's most famous stores, Harrods lives up to its motto, *Omnia Omnibus Ubique*—everything, for everyone, everywhere. Though the store might not be so unabashedly sumptuous as in times past, it still reigns supreme among British department stores, especially the astounding food halls. Don't miss the extensive and exotic selections, the elaborate displays —the seafood arrangement, in particular, is stunning—and the breathtaking floor, wall, and ceiling tiles.

Harrods is popular with many members of the Royal Family;

the Princes William and Harry come here at Christmas to sit on Santa's lap, though they are naturally spared the long lines. But don't be misled into thinking you might rub shoulders with the Queen—whenever she visits the 15-acre store, it opens an hour early just for her.

Harvey Nichols

Knightsbridge
London SW1X 7RJ
(01–235 5000).

Linen drapers to HM The Queen, drapers to HM The Queen Mother, and suppliers of household and fancy goods to HRH The Prince of Wales.

Harvey Nichols is one of the best and most impressive department stores in London, renowned for the superlative quality and range of its goods, from household furnishings and stationery to jewelry and the latest fashions. The Princess of Wales has often been seen shopping at this supremely chic shop. A good alternative to Harrods if you can't take crowds.

Liberty

Regent Street
London W1R 6AH
(01–734 1234)

Silk mercers to HM The Queen Mother.

Situated off Regent Street and just down from Oxford Circus, Liberty is probably best known and loved for its exceptional Liberty fabrics, from vibrant paisleys and exuberant florals to restrained Art Deco motifs. The store itself is beautifully decorated, and the neo-Tudor facade is a delight. For tasteful gifts, visit the accessory section on the ground floor, its counters brimming with Liberty prints and designer handkerchiefs, scarves, and shawls, plus fabric-bound objects such as notebooks, diaries, and picture frames. The Oriental and ethnic sections are intriguing, with their wide range of unusual items. The glass department stocks some lovely Venetian perfume bottles and the like. Altogether, this is an elegant and highly discriminating department store.

Moyses Steven

6 Bruton Street
London W1X 7AG
(01–493 8171)

Florists to HM The Queen Mother.
This suitably regal shop put together Princess Anne's wedding bouquet. It also supplies flowers and floral arrangements to several foreign royal families.

Thomas Goode & Company
19 South Audley Street
London W1Y 6BN
(01–499 2823)
Suppliers of china and glass to HM The Queen, HM The Queen Mother, and HRH The Prince of Wales.
A must for collectors of china or lovers of beautiful things, this old-established shop has over a dozen showrooms displaying the finest china, crystal, and ornamental items by such firms as Spode, Royal Worcester, Waterford, Minton, and Baccarat. One room contains a collection of china animals much patronized by the Princess of Wales, who collects china owls and rabbits.

ROYAL RECREATION

Hatchards
187–188 Piccadilly
London W1V 9DA
(01–439 9921)
Booksellers to HM The Queen, HM The Queen Mother, HRH The Duke of Edinburgh, and HRH The Prince of Wales.
This is the only London bookshop to be granted a royal warrant, and it distances itself further from its competitors by having collected all four, a remarkable feat. Occupying an elegant building opposite the Royal Academy, it stocks everything from children's to rare books (and even some rare children's books). Hatchards created a royal first when Princess Michael of Kent accepted the store's invitation to hold a public signing session of her controversial book *Born in a Far Country*. Interest was so great that traffic in Piccadilly was brought to an impatient halt for several hours.

Holland & Holland
33 Bruton Street
London W1X 8JS
(01–499 4411)

Rifle makers to HRH The Duke of Edinburgh.

Holland & Holland will make a new gun or alter one of its secondhand guns to a client's individual requirements, taking into account height, width, fullness of face, and length of neck. You can also buy shooting clothes and accessories at this supremely sporting shop.

James Purdey & Sons

Audley House
57–58 South Audley Street
London W1Y 6ED
(01–499 1801)

Gun and cartridge makers to HM The Queen and HRH The Prince of Wales, and gunmakers to HRH The Duke of Edinburgh.

England's Royal Family has been using Purdey guns and rifles for six generations—from the days of Queen Victoria. The guns are works of art, the top of the line in the shooting world. They are made to the customer's personal measurements and sporting requirements to ensure that each is an extension of the shooter's arm. The firm also stocks a complete range of shooting clothes and accessories. A Purdey gun commands a hefty price tag, but you will undoubtedly get what you pay for—at least, that's what proud owners say.

John Rigby & Company

66 Great Suffolk Street
Southwark
London SE1 0BV
(01–620 0690)

Rifle and cartridge makers to HM The Queen.

This ultra-conservative company was awarded its first royal warrant by Queen Victoria, but has royal connections going back to 1735, when it was established during the reign of George II. Today, its rifles are used by the Queen during the deer-stalking season at her Scottish home, Balmoral.

Lillywhites

Piccadilly Circus
London SW1Y 4QF
(01–930 3181)

Outfitters to HM The Queen.

Lillywhites is the largest single sporting goods retailer in the country, selling equipment and accessories for just about every sport known to man. Today Lillywhites supplies the younger members of the Royal Family with skiing outfits for their annual winter sports vacation in Klosters, Switzerland. It also supplies the British team at the Winter Olympics. It designed the aviation suit worn by Amy Johnson on her solo flight to Australia, and the first pair of tennis shorts worn at Wimbledon.

Maggs Brothers
50 Berkeley Square
London W1X 6EL
(01–493 7160)
Purveyors of rare books and manuscripts to HM The Queen.
The interior of this elegant Georgian house in Berkeley Square has the look and feel of a private library, with its glass-fronted bookcases reaching up to the ceiling, crammed full of rare volumes. The shop also sells historical documents, plus autographs of the famous, both past and present.

ROYAL RESTAURANTS _____

Claridge's
Brook Street
London W1A 2JQ
(01–629 8860)
Claridge's is one of the great London hotels, with particularly strong links with the Royal Family. The Queen has given a number of highly select parties here, most notably on the evening of Prince Charles and Princess Diana's wedding. The Duchess of York and her father, Major Ronald Ferguson, are also regular visitors. The food is mainly French, the decor superb, the service impeccable.

Langan's Brasserie
Stratton Street
London W1X 5FD
(01–493 6437)
This smart eatery has become a meeting place of royalty and show-business stars alike; it's undoubtedly one of *the* places to be seen in London. Prince Michael, Princess Margaret, Viscount Linley, Lady Helen Windsor, the Duke of York, and Lord Snowdon all dine here on the superb French fare.

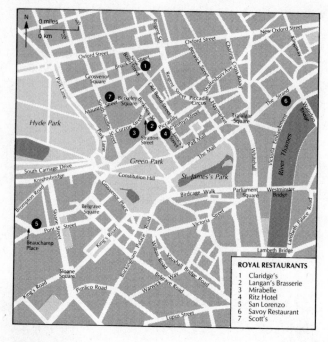

ROYAL RESTAURANTS
1 Claridge's
2 Langan's Brasserie
3 Mirabelle
4 Ritz Hotel
5 San Lorenzo
6 Savoy Restaurant
7 Scott's

Mirabelle

56 Curzon Street
London W1Y 8DL
(01–499 4636)

In the throbbing heart of Mayfair, the Mirabelle is near the royal
hairdressers, Trumpers, and opposite the headquarters of M15
(Britain's version of the CIA). Princess Margaret, Viscount Althorp (the Princess of Wales's brother), Lady Fermoy (their
grandmother), the Duchess of York, Prince Rupert Lowenstein,
and many other foreign royals are often seen in this sophisticated restaurant enjoying its fine cuisine.

Ritz Hotel

Piccadilly
London W1V 9DG
(01–493 8181)

The "world's most fashionable hotel" has always been popular
with the Royal Family, offering, as it does, polished (if somewhat pompous) service in sumptuous surroundings. Afternoon

tea—book ahead—in the Palm Court is an eye-opening experience, and you will undoubtedly find yourself in company with the cream of London society.

San Lorenzo
22 Beauchamp Place
London SW3 1NH
(01–584 1074)
Just a stone's throw from Harrods, this chic Italian restaurant is another meeting place for the rich and famous, such as Jane Fonda, Sylvester Stallone, Mick Jagger, Rod Stewart, and Walter Matthau. It is also a great favorite of the Princess of Wales, the Duchess of York, Viscount Linley, and Lady Sarah Armstrong-Jones.

Savoy Hotel
The Strand
London WC2R 0EU
(01–836 4343)
The Savoy has long been one of London's most prestigious hotels, and is appropriately popular with the Royal Family, especially Princess Margaret. Head for the River Room restaurant. The service is discreetly courteous, the surroundings sumptuous, and the food magnificent.

Scott's
20 Mount Street
London W1Y 6HE
(01–629 5248)
Scott's is one of the city's most royal of royal restaurants. This highly lauded Mayfair eating place is another favorite of the Duchess of York, who often lunches here with her employer, publisher Richard Burton, or with girlfriends.

ROYAL SCOTLAND

Countrywear
15 Bridge Street
Ballater
Aberdeenshire AB3 5QP, Scotland
(0338–55453)
Sporting outfitters to HM The Queen, HM The Queen Mother, and HRH The Prince of Wales.

Awarded its first royal warrant by Queen Victoria and its latest by the Prince of Wales, this postage stamp of a shop is festooned with royal crests. Countrywear stocks exceptionally well-made traditional Scottish clothing—including an excellent selection of tweed jackets—as well as many types of traditional country sporting and leisure equipment.

J. & D. Murray

10 Bridge Street
Ballater
Aberdeenshire AB3 5QP, Scotland
(0338–55409)

Chemists to HM The Queen and HM The Queen Mother.

J. & D. Murray's most popular preparation is Ironside's Emollient Skin Cream, which has been much in demand for over 50 years. Mr. Murray also invented a deliciously scented aftershave known as Highland Fern, and two delicate perfumes—Balmoral Mist and Dee Heather.

Jenners

48 Princes Street
Edinburgh EH2 2YJ, Scotland
(031–225 2442)

Suppliers of furnishing materials to HM The Queen.

The facade of this impressive building shows a pleasing mixture of Jacobean and French architectural styles, while inside you will be confronted by the lovely Grand Hall with its mahogany counters, marble floors, and tiered galleries. Jenners holds the royal warrant to supply furnishing fabrics to the Queen for her Scottish residences of Balmoral and Holyroodhouse. With a reputation as a decidedly upper-crust sort of shop—it's the world's oldest independent department store—Jenners stocks merchandise of only the most exacting quality. The fashion departments—for men, women, and children—are notable, as is the first-rate china and glass selection.

Kinloch Anderson

John Knox House
45 High Street
Edinburgh EH11 1SR, Scotland
(031–556 6961)

Tailors and kiltmakers to HM The Queen, HRH The Duke of Edinburgh, and HRH The Prince of Wales.

If you want an authentic Scottish kilt to wear to your next costume party or caber-tossing tournament, this is the shop to head for. It also sells sporrans—the furry purses worn over the kilt—traditional jewelry, and a range of classic women's clothing based on Scottish designs.

Index

INDEX

Map references are found in **boldface**.